# THE 7 STEPS TO HELP YOUR SON IN ADDICTION RECOVERY

UNDERSTANDING ADDICTIONS AS ROOTED IN TRAUMA, AND HOW YOUR SON WILL RECOVER

DORCAS WANGANGA

(HEALTH COACH)

# CONTENTS

## STEP #3
### NOURISH YOUR SPIRIT WITH SELF-CARE

## STEP #4
### COMMUNICATION

# Just      for      You!

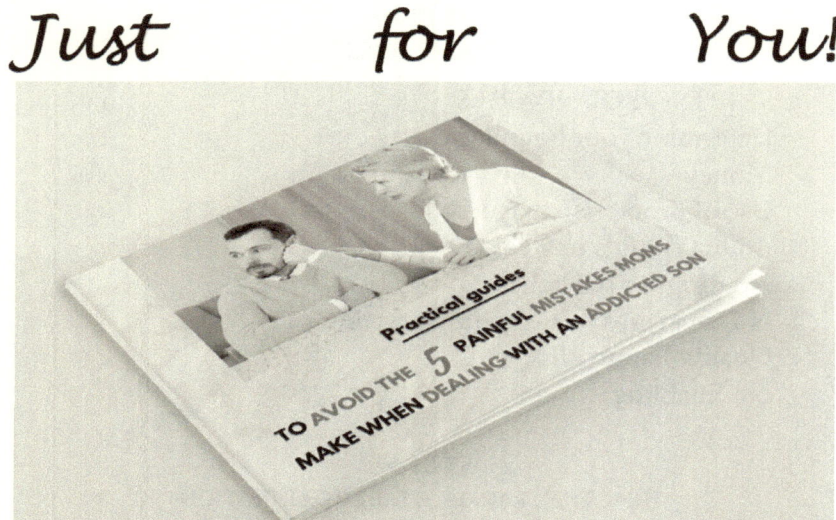

*A gift for all moms who purchase this book. Practical guides to practice daily and avoid painful mistakes as you seek to help your son.*

*To get your copy go to*
*newstarttohealth.com*

# INTRODUCTION

I was chatting with my friend Cindy when she burst out, "I am just about ready to kick him out. I have tried everything; I don't know my son anymore. He is rude, aggressive, irresponsible, and every conversation I try to have with him turns into an argument or complete shutdown. Last night he even slammed the door in my face after I asked him why he was coming in late, yet school had been over for hours. He doesn't spend time with Jason anymore; I thought Jason was his best friend! He has been spending hours either locked up in his room or out with God knows who, and his room looks like a tornado just passed through it."

As I listened sympathetically, she ranted on.

"His grades have dropped, he is no longer motivated to do anything, he is rude, and everything I say gets twisted around, I get yelled at or ignored. The last time I gave him an ultimatum, he said he hated me. I have never felt more hurt in my life. My life is a nightmare!"

"I am tense all the time; his father does not seem to care. I am at my wit's end. I have prayed, begged, threatened, and my son just seems to be getting worse. Just what happened to my child? He seemed happy, bright, friendly, and intelligent growing up. I see all that somewhere in him, but right now, he has turned into a stranger. I panic when I don't see him; anxiety has been my constant companion, I barely sleep, and I feel like my whole life revolves around my baby. He is surely using something. I'm not sure what, although I had seen some cigarette butts outside. But cigarettes don't make you like this. Or do they? I thought I caught a whiff of weed on his breath yesterday, Aargh!"

Sound familiar? Cindy's experience above may well be one of the thousands of moms whose teen and young adult sons struggle with addiction. For a mother, her most precious treasure is her child, and it is not just the most incredible gift but a great responsibility. When I talk with other moms facing the same problem, all their stories are almost similar. They speak of the helplessness, frustration, and the feeling that they lost control of their teen or young adult sons and cannot see how the disconnect happened. Some do and blame themselves; others are riddled with guilt and try to do the best they can to help fix the problem, while others are angry and broken and feel like their child has reached the point of no return.

The Bible says,

> *"Lo, children are an heritage of the LORD, and the fruit of the womb is His reward."*

— PSALMS 127:3

Then why does it seem like the opposite is true?

One mom said to me, "My son Kevin was the sweetest boy growing up. He was everything a parent would want; he had good grades, was active, had good friends, and was kind to everyone. He was a great kid. But my baby is now a shadow of the child I raised and love. A lot changed in just a few months; I hate addiction! Honestly, my world has literally fallen apart."

Around the world, mothers are facing a similar problem. Raising a person, giving them all the love, wisdom, and knowledge they will need to face the world, is way more complicated than birthing one. Yet every day, parents are expected to create the ideal environment for their child's proper physical and mental growth. For undeniable reasons, that is not always possible to provide. But we try. Every mother tries her best to raise her kids with love and affection: even the seemingly worst mothers, moms who may have abused their kids.

However, some bad experiences may be impossible to prevent. Let's say you have done everything you can to ensure a happy childhood for your son. You have given him a good home, a good education, and loving parents. Even then, for some reason or event unknown to you, he may be suffering from mental trauma. Remember, no one is immune from the claws of substance abuse. Even the seemingly happy teen can succumb to depression and sadness and turn to drugs.

Furthermore, our society is becoming more averse to a healthy childhood. Did you know one of the biggest threats to your child in 21st century America is addiction? One study on eight public schools and around one thousand 9th grade students shows that about 9% take marijuana, 3% take heroin, and 21% take opioids. The actual numbers behind these percentages are even scarier. A study showed that about 881,000 kids between the age of 12-17 years were using non-prescribed opioids in the US in 2016. The numbers have multiplied since then, and it is a nationwide crisis.

For children who have experienced trauma in childhood, this rate is even higher. A recent report published in 2021 shows the close relationship between childhood adversity, early-life stress, alcohol, and drug addiction. According to the research, *"Higher severity and frequency of childhood trauma"* are almost always associated with increased substance abuse habits.

Knowing that your son is abusing substances is a nightmare. One cannot fathom the confusion, frustration, anger, and helplessness a parent goes through when they find out. For some, the very thought is unthinkable. I was one of those parents who blissfully lived in this vacuum. I was naive to believe that my work was done because I had given "the talk" on the dangers of drugs and alcohol. My son had assured me that he would never be involved in this kind of behavior. However, no matter how unlikely it seems, it is more common than most people think, and as a mom, the best thing you can do is understand the enemy and develop strategies to fight back.

Any child is vulnerable; it may not be substance use, but other addictions that we shall discuss later are just as destructive. Some signs like sudden mood changes, temper flares, sleep changes, weight gain or loss, constant red eyes, isolation, disinterest in activities he loved before, lack of motivation, etc., are glaring indications of substance abuse or behavioral addictions. You may have noticed these changes but, before you could address them effectively, things quickly got out of hand, and now your attempts to resolve them have not worked. It could be the reason you have this book, *The 7 Steps to Help Your Son in Addiction Recovery,* in your hands today, and I sincerely believe it will be a great help to you.

"But what else should I do when my son is abusing substances or engaged in risky behavior after I have done everything I can to help?" You may ask.

Unfortunately, there are no pre-written, precise steps to follow, no specific treatment patterns when it comes to addictions. The road to recovery is long and disheartening. It's a marathon that will drain you, hurt you, test your patience, and make you doubt everything, including yourself. The worst part? There are very few tools to guide you. Sure, you can send your son to therapy or rehab, but what about your role as a mom? Exactly how are you to approach him and make him accept your help? You will agree with me just how hard it is to cope, help him, and stay sane at the same time. That is precisely why you have this book, to be your guide and friend in these dark times.

By now, we can assume that the pain and heartbreak you have suffered so far is nothing compared to what may lie ahead. Every mother I have encountered is afraid of what may happen to her son. Is it heartbreak, poor school or job performance, jail, death? Hidden beneath the pain and suffering is hope. You know you can rescue your son, and that's why you haven't given up. By understanding him, helping him, healing the pain and sadness he is desperately trying to mask with substances, you can slowly and surely bring him back. It's a long journey, but it is doable!

I got the inspiration to write because I have been through a similar journey. My son's substance abuse was the worst thing that happened to me. I went from shock to depression, rage, sadness, and a feeling of helplessness- I was devastated. Slowly I got up with determination; I wasn't going to let this enemy win. And knowing I am not the only one who has felt lost and confused, I got on the journey.

I spent time in prayer, claiming God's promises.

> *Thus saith the Lord; "Refrain thy voice from weeping, and thine eyes from tears: for thy work shall be rewarded, saith the Lord; and they shall come again from the land of the enemy. And there is hope in thine end, saith the Lord, that thy children shall come again to their own border."*
>
> — JEREMIAH 31:16-7

I solicited the prayer of brethren, family, and friends and sought wisdom to deal with this situation. And I can gladly say that God has come through for me in more ways than one. I know many mothers who faced the exact bleak times but were determined to bring their loved ones back from the claws of addiction. Some have had success stories, and I have seen them; some have been left bereft, while others are still on the battlefield. This book is an attempt to provide more tools for battle.

Now, I will not claim to be an expert in either addiction or neurobiology. But I am someone who has experienced extreme pain and fear for a child who does not seem to realize whence he is treading. I have put in writing a collection of the understanding and wisdom I have gained on this journey while helping him. It's an attempt to leave my knowledge so the next mother does not have to suffer the extreme pain of following the wrong path. In short, it's a book written by one hurting mother to another.

I cited peer-reviewed journal articles for making this book as accurate and helpful as possible. If there were a time people needed to review what they know and approach addiction, it is now. The *7 Steps to Help Your Son in Addiction Recovery* is not just a book to tell you the seven steps to quit the addiction. No! any website or therapy pamphlet can do that. This book seeks to go deeper than that. We will explore your son's possible experiences, probe the root of his addictions, and seek to help him and you as well.

With The *7 Steps to Help Your Son in Addiction Recovery,* you are about to embark on a journey that is not commonly trodden, a compassionate look at an addict's struggles, and empathy to a mother who gets addicted to the addiction. It will highlight the importance of understanding the user, or one involved in risky behavior, and awareness of the specific advice that goes against what a mother believes to be true or God's teachings on relationships. You will find peace, strength, and hope.

This book aims to help you

- Get rid of all the negativity, self-doubt, frustration, and anger you feel towards the whole situation.
- Forgive and recover yourself and your son.
- Rebuild the beautiful relationship you desire with him.

In this book, I am speaking with the *mother of a son or sons* not to discriminate against other parents or caretakers, but to personalize it for you, the mom with a son. Otherwise, it is for every mother, father, grandparent, or caregiver with a teen or young adult son or daughter. It is for anyone struggling to help their child, but all the advice received so far either feels wrong or has not worked.

I cringe every time someone says, 'Kick him out..." and while I know this may be the only option most moms may have, my motherly instincts recoil at the thought as I know yours do. I desire and pray that you will use this book often with a realization that nothing comes easy. Rebuilding trust and relationships take time, but if you are the mom I know you are, you got this! So go on! Keep the faith and hope, for God has promised:

> *"For I know the thoughts I think toward you, saith*
> *The Lord, thoughts of peace; and not of evil, to*
> *give you an expected end."*

> — JEREMIAH 29:11

# STEP #1

## UNDERSTANDING ADDICTIONS

# KNOW YOUR ENEMY

During my research, I came across a true story of a mom; let's call her Julia, whose son progressed from opioids, heroin to meth addiction. According to Julia, her son Roy was a happy kid, polite, good in school, no trouble, loved sports, a go-getter, and was not afraid to try new things. In the story, the boy lost his best friend at a young age, which devastated him. Almost overnight, his behavior changed drastically. He was treated for depression, and the medications impaired him so much that he could sleep for hours, yet they did not work. Later Roy had an accident and broke his collarbone. His doctor prescribed Vicodin, an opiate, and he got hooked despite his mom's attempt to deter him. Looking back, Julia realized that her son was predisposed to addiction, having come from a family of addicts, including his dad. And thus started the roller coaster ride of recoveries and relapses. The judge sentenced him to house arrest, which he violated, juvenile since he was a minor, rehab, but all these attempts failed, and he had several relapses.

You are probably shaking your head in sympathy, seeing a familiar pattern in this story. Because it could be you, or someone you knew, even before your child was involved. Maybe it was an uncle, the neighbor's son, or even the janitor in your office. Did you ever wonder about their condition? Why had they got into that situation in the first place? When I found that my son was using substances, I was devastated. Like any other mom, I struggled with grief, anger, and disappointment. Then came the guilt that almost crushed me. I blamed myself for things I was not sure had anything to do with the situation. Many nights I woke up in a sweat, panic in my throat. For many days I hoped to wake up from the nightmare, which I thought would never end.

However, praise God because as I was going through these emotions, sometimes getting really angry, I had the mind to step back, seeking to understand my son better. So, I spent sleepless nights praying and pleading with God for direction. I needed to understand what led him to this path, and thus I started my research. I would be lying if I said this was an easy path, and more so if I implied I had an easy solution or a solution at all. I kept in mind that not all moms reading this book are able to help their sons, but I believe any caretaker can find plenty of helpful information that will direct them to know what they are contending with.

Knowing the enemy involves the awareness that your son's habit and ensuing behavior is not the enemy. He did not roll out one day and decide to make your life a living hell, as he ruined his and everyone else's in the home. It was a process that took time. Understanding addiction will help you identify the enemy to fight and the tools you need to win.

In Roy's case, some glaring issues that could have led him to addiction came up. One of his parents was an alcoholic. Usually, this environment can be traumatic for a child; he experienced a devastating loss at a young age. He was offered a solution for his emotional and physical pain through prescription. To a troubled teenage boy whose brain is still developing, this is like manna from heaven.

# THE ROLLER COASTER

By regular people like you and me, addiction is rarely understood. It is unknown. Nay! the existence of addiction has always been known. However, even after all these years, addiction is hardly spoken about or discussed in everyday conversation. We know it exists. We know it is affecting many people in our community, yet we ignore this glaring problem. Happy to sweep it under the rug unless someone we love suffers from this terrible condition. After all, no mother would ever imagine her loving son as anything but ordinary and happy. Yet so many of the young are falling victim to it. They are misinformed, misunderstood, and cast away. They struggle to cope with what they are going through and are too afraid, ashamed, or guilty to go to a mom who has a limited understanding of the problem.

As you can imagine, even if the teen or young adult son is trying to get help from the parents, the conversations usually do not go well. Most mothers instantly try to help, but as they do not fully understand the condition, they get frustrated, anxious, depressed, and sometimes enraged; it is a very emotional situation. They don't know why their son cannot just give up this risky behavior. "Does he not get that using substances will destroy his life?" On the other hand, the son doesn't comprehend why his mom does not understand his struggle. He may feel trapped between his desire to please her and the guilt, shame, and helplessness towards the pull of the addiction.

Dr. Gabor Maté (BA, MD) explains that to some addicts, the high of drugs feels like a warm hug from a loved one, making them feel comfortable and safe instead of isolated.

Suppose he feels judged, criticized, or misunderstood? Then he withdraws more from those who love him, avoids his parents or interaction with family and friends by skipping dinner, spending more time isolated in his room or out with questionable friends, as he could be fearful of more confrontations. Evil sees its opportunity when a child feels isolated from loved ones, deprived of warmth and love. This emotional alienation pushes him even deeper into the claws of addiction. However, as a mom, the desire to fix this problem grows in magnitude.

Julia said it was a roller coaster ride, days of recovery, relapse, overdosing, and jail; she lost her peace. Yet, there was no way she could give up on her young son. She saw him try, even admit himself into treatment, and she supported him as best as she could. Eventually, she went to parents' support meetings and learned to change her approach to help Roy. In the narrative, he was not out of the woods yet, but she had learned how to help him better.

You may have received all kinds of advice from other struggling moms, experts, spouses, relatives and may have tried to follow through, only to see things get worse. You may have enabled him by providing everything he asked for, and some he didn't, out of guilt or to appease him, but as time went by, you realized the approach was not working, and the situation was escalating. It will not be a surprise if you have asked yourself, "What does work? When even the slightest confrontation or a simple mention about addiction seems to trigger your son, he disappears and stays stuck in his room for hours or gets violent or so angry that he yells profanities in your face and disappears from home for several days. Things like these have made moms make seemingly callous decisions. There is also the guilt, helplessness, and frustrations that arise from the escalating situation. It takes strength and courage mingled with fear to kick a child out of home, yet it has turned into an option for most moms; how heartbreaking!

And then, after some days, he does communicate, seems contrite, and you are relieved, happy to see him only for your hopes to be dashed again. It almost seems like he intentionally wants to hurt you. I mean, why can't he just quit this habit? I am sure you have had this thought or conversation many times. Perhaps after you confronted him about his use or behavior or after taking some privileges like the Wi-Fi or his phone from him, he may have agreed to quit at some point. Then the behaviors would materialize, and you would be incredibly frustrated and perplexed at your son's "selfishness." After all, things were just turning around! Why would he go back again? Or why did he start in the first place? You know you taught him better, raised him better. So, it is very natural to be exasperated. While the cycle does not seem to end, any mom must be entirely drained to quit the battle.

So, as stated earlier, the first step in battling addiction and even preventing it is knowing the enemy. And we all know who the enemy of humanity is. God promised,

> *"But thus saith The LORD, even the captives of the mighty shall be taken away, and the prey of the terrible shall be diverted: for I will contend with him that contendeth with thee, and I will save thy children."*

> — ISAIAH 49:25

The Creator made us his best creation and blessed us with children. He gave us life and sent us holy scripts to live our lives happily and fully. Contrary to what the Almighty wanted, Satan insinuated himself, and parents neglected their responsibility to prioritize family. However, God has promised to contend with the enemy and save our children. Addiction is one of the enemies that seem to roll from one generation to another, to where most experts claim it to be genetic. It has destroyed families, torn them apart, and closed the door against the Holy Spirit. Professionals are still battling for better ways to eradicate it.

God established the family unit to symbolize the relationship we humans should have with Him, our Redeemer. And it was to be a happy, closely knit, loving family environment. But from the beginning, it was Satan's concerted desire to destroy this harmony in the home, and he has succeeded on a large scale from the pain we know is experienced in many homes behind closed doors. These days there are more attacks on families than ever. There are higher divorce rates, domestic violence, more trauma, coldness in the heart, and more children born to single parents. No matter how you look at it, there is a concerning number of failing and broken families in all communities. Media trends, substance abuse, and a tendency toward breaking lifelong commitments have gripped the world. But it is undeniable that in these trying times, the bonds of God and family can be the savior of individuals.

To battle addiction, one needs strong connections, great relationships, and purpose in life. So, prepare to take this journey, holding on with the hand of faith, defying Satan's effort and regaining your sanity, recovering your son, reuniting your family, and ending the roller coaster.

# 3

# WHAT IS ADDICTION?

Addiction is defined in many ways. It was assumed to be a disease for many years. According to the National Institute of Drug Abuse (NIDA,) *"Addiction is defined as a chronic, relapsing brain disease that is characterized by uncontrollable drug seeking and use, despite detrimental consequences."* There is much disagreement among experts on whether addiction can be called a disease or not. Those who called addiction a chronic disease believed that they could successfully treat it with medications and rehabs. They could explain why some individuals were more prone to falling prey to addictive substances while others were not.

When viewed as a disease, addiction supports the general assumption that a substance abuser lacks morality or is uncaring of the consequences of his actions—accepting it as such allows pharmaceuticals to develop more drugs to reduce withdrawals and improve the quality of life. The most convincing reason to call it a disease is that addiction changes how people's brains work. And it is not only minor changes either; one immensely significant part of the brain is entirely "rewired" after a specific amount of time has passed. (Yet, the brain is inherently changeable. Any experience, bad or good, changes the brain. It is a trait of brain tissue called "Neuroplasticity")

As the research is pouring in, written by doctors dealing with addicts, it is becoming clear that the disease label is losing its hold. The addict cannot be treated with medication (not wholly) unless there is an underlying mental illness. There is no apparent direct pathological cause of it, nor is there any straightforward method that applies to all addicts in general as diseases tend to have. Instead, as complex as addiction is, most psychiatrists nowadays treat addiction as a response to a person's emotional status or even habits and mental conditions that have developed over time.

According to one textbook definition," *Substance addiction is a neuropsychiatric disorder characterized by a constant desire to continue taking the drug despite dire consequences.*" In a paper published in January 2011, Dr. Marc Lewis of the University of Toronto explored the possible definitions of addiction. In this paper, he explained that addiction to substances, like others in behavioral, is more of a habit or even a brain condition. This paper started a decade-long debate of how to define addiction.

All addiction, including behavioral, changes how the brain responds to various stimuli. People who become substance abusers sought out the habit in the first place because it gave them relief from pain or offered temporary elation, joy, or as an escape from their emotional distress.

The problem with addiction is that this feeling of happiness or satisfaction is stimulated and controlled by a neuromodulator named dopamine. Why is that a problem? See, dopamine is produced in the brain as a reaction to good things happening, mainly rewarding behaviors. For example, when you get a long-desired job or a pair of shoes as a gift, you get an increased dopamine secretion in your brain. In medical words, dopamine is a neurotransmitter that controls motivating, directing, and rewarding goal-directed behavior and focusing attention and memory. Thus, dopamine does not only control feeling good but also controls behavior regarding those activities. So, when one uses substances, it invariably takes over all these behaviors as well.

My favorite definition of addiction is "*any behavior, substance-related or not, that an individual pursues because they find pleasure, relief, or they crave it temporarily, so they pursue pleasure and relief despite negative consequences.*" Any act that provides an individual relief and pleasure can induce addiction, such as shopping, work, sex, substance, etc. All of it can stimulate the dopamine rush and conditioned learning we just discussed.

Although not discussed in everyday conversations, addiction is prevalent. However, the pharmacology of drugs and alcohol renders it more potent than any non-substance addiction. Most drugs used by addicts are central nervous system stimulants or depressants, painkillers, and psychedelics, all with one thing in common; they induce tolerance and dependence. Dependence is a dangerous property of some pharmacological substances. It means that these pharmacologically active substances cause compulsions to take the drug to experience its psychic effect or to avoid the discomfort of the absence of its effects. Dependence results from changes at a molecular level and is not only in the "mind" as some people will often say addiction is.

However, the process of all addiction development is pretty much the same. Even the changes in the brain are primarily of the same type; shopping or eating addictions can become worse than drugs and alcohol addictions in some cases. Although the basis of developing the habit stays the same, there is a social stigma against drugs and alcohol so much so that parents and general society don't put them into the same category.

A cigarette habit is regular and may be expected in a grown man. Marijuana use? Frowned upon perhaps, but legal in most states now. But cocaine is still strictly illegal and still considered a hard drug. So, why do some drugs raise the alarm, and some don't? It is because of pharmacological dependence and tolerance. While dependence means the person taking the drug feels the vital need to use it to prevent withdrawal symptoms, tolerance is the opposite.

Tolerance means the drug loses the severity of its effect with repeated use as the brain cell receptors become "tolerant" to its stimulation. This adds to the addictive effect of the drug as the person using it has to increase the amount he uses each time to reach the same level of euphoria.

That's why a substance abuser may end up abusing more than one type of drug. For example, our friend Roy was using opioids because they made him feel happy and relieved. He could not let go of this feeling because he had never felt this way before. It was a relief to ease the emotional turmoil he felt at the loss of his friend, as well as the physical pain from the broken collarbone. Who knows, maybe he had a bad experience with his alcoholic father growing up. But he later transitioned to cocaine and then meth as the effects of the opioids were not as potent anymore. Understanding these mechanisms helps us appreciate just how much "good" they can make a person feel.

Each substance induces different levels of dependency and tolerance and creates different levels of "potency" of addiction. However, a person's dependence does not always mean that he is addicted, especially regarding prescriptions.

While there are several explanations for why this process starts and why people develop addictions, Dr. Gabor Maté emphasizes that it is not necessarily the drugs that cause the addiction. However, he does agree that some elements need to be in place for addiction to occur. These include a susceptible organism, meaning someone vulnerable; a drug with addictive potential; and toxic stress. If a highly susceptible person is under stress and has drugs available, there is a high chance he will get hooked, as we saw in Roy's case.

# 4

# THE DEVELOPING BRAIN

I t is a Christian family, and all of Jade's children grew up playing musical instruments. Her son Edward who she fondly calls "Ed," loved playing the piano, guitar, and violin. People in church always looked forward to worship music time because he played the piano beautifully; he was very talented. Lately, Jade has sadly watched as Ed's friend Kim took Ed's place since Ed does not attend church anymore.

Most of the time, she doesn't know where he spends his days and nights as his life has been consumed by cocaine. They have tried rehab several times, and he always relapses. Honestly, she doesn't know what else he uses, but she says her child is a total stranger and rarely talks anymore. Of all her four children, she always thought he was the brightest and most talented, but not so anymore. They all pray that someday he will be released from this bondage and come back to the fold.

Addiction is a reaction to negative experiences earlier in life or even current conditions. As in Ed's case, the mother, Jade, often blamed herself, remembering how depressed she was when Ed was a baby and how she sometimes did not have the energy or patience with his incessant crying. Could that have affected his brain? While we cannot speculate, we know that it can be a way Ed tries to cope with emotional deprivation.

These stories are almost similar, but one thing is clear; the utter helplessness a mom experiences, and the question is almost always the same? "Why my son, dear Lord?" "How did this start?"

Understanding how addiction begins is just the tip of the iceberg, but what happens in the brain of an addict?

According to studies, the brain is the most complex of all the human body organs, and no one can fully claim to understand how it works. It has more than 86 billion neurons that communicate to share circuits and information. It can also malfunction in various ways causing disorders that impact people socially and economically.

The origin of addiction is mostly trauma or painful experiences, often in childhood. But why in childhood? How can something that happened in the past have such an immense effect on the present? The reason becomes clear once you understand brain development. Humans and all other animals develop from a single cell, and this single cell divides into several and creates three germ layers, giving rise to organs and systems. You see, the various systems that make up our body were once all combined. Different parts of the brain, for example, are developed from the same type of neuronal tissues and are constantly interacting with each other. So, it is not surprising that your emotions, which result from stimulation of the part of the brain for creating feelings, have a tangible, measurable effect on other parts of the brain.

These effects are there at every stage of life, but the results are lasting on a child's developing brain. As the brain is still forming, any negative or positive emotions create changes in the brain cells that last a lifetime. For example, when interacting with parents, a well-loved nurtured and happy child experiences a rush of endorphins, a natural opioid. As a result, a good number of dopamine receptors are formed in his brain. At the same time, another child that does not have a happy childhood never experiences a rush of endorphins due to lack of warmth and care, or even worse emotional or physical abuse from caretakers.

These stressful circumstances lead to the formation of very few dopamine and opioid receptors. These receptors later determine a person's vulnerability to addiction. Because the low receptors mean they need a high dose of dopamine to create a normal level of happiness. One study found that mice with lower dopamine and opioid receptors were more likely to get addicted to cocaine. The same goes for people. Children who are less happy in childhood and always feel anxious, edgy, and unhappy develop fewer dopamine receptors. When these kids take drugs for the first time, they get a huge dopamine rush like they have never experienced before. Suddenly they are calm, happy, and in control. This feeling of peace, this high, is what gets them hooked.

The quality and the quantity of time spent with the parents also matter. Studies show that an infant's stress levels are directly related to the amount of maternal interaction. Suppose an infant is deprived of maternal contact? He will have a dangerously high cortisol level (the stress hormone), vasopressin (high blood pressure), and low oxytocin and serotonin levels. These hormones are crucial for development and can lead to severe malformation of brain tissues like shrinkage of the hippocampus and imbalance of several pathways.

According to a paper published by Dr. Gabor Maté, an addiction expert, author, and speaker, *"A child's ability to handle psychological and physiological stress is totally dependent on the relationship with their parents. Infants cannot regulate their stress apparatus, leading to death due to stress if they are never picked up or held. This capacity is acquired gradually through maturation and is dependent on relationships with caregivers."*

Hundreds of studies have proven that the presence of "bad" experiences during childhood affects a person's brain development just as severely as the absence of "good" experiences.

Toxic stress in childhood establishes a lower "set point" for his internal stress system: he gets stressed far more quickly than an average person due to the culmination of the childhood traumas that he experienced. One study shows that the brains of mistreated children are smaller than usual by 7 or 8 % with the smaller impulse-regulating prefrontal cortex.

Another study showed that the hippocampus (the memory and emotional hub) was 15 % smaller in women who were abused as children. Another one shows that in the EEGs (a test to check the brain's electrical activity) of adults who had been sexually abused, the majority had abnormal brainwaves, and over a third showed seizure activity. So, scientifically, children who go through abuse or other forms of trauma have difficulty managing their emotions; they are more likely to develop depression and have an anatomical brain structure that makes them more vulnerable to addiction. However, some people can go through immense emotional trauma and still live ordinary everyday lives.

# 5

# AT CELLULAR LEVEL

As a child grows, his brain also grows, and the development often mirrors the experiences he has while growing up. The truth is, the brain is constantly changing. New connections or "synapses" between neurons are built daily, while old and unused ones get lost. Think of it like "trails" on fields. One can easily create a new trail or path on an area by simply walking along it a few times. And just as quickly, old tracks get covered with grass when no one walks on them anymore. Synapses are like that. Well-used routes or synapses that transfer stimuli repeatedly get stronger over time; the transfer time gets shorter. And the synapses or connections that have no stimuli to transfer get lost. Neurologists use two terms to explain this: synaptic growth and synaptic pruning.

Synaptic growth happens when you take a new path, meaning when you learn a new skill or do a new thing and memorize it. Like in the case of Ed, he had learned how to play the piano from repeatedly practicing as he grew up. So, when a person is frequently using substances, the synapses associated with that get more robust.

Synaptic pruning is a process that begins in infancy to adulthood when the brain naturally removes connections that are no longer in use. It is a mechanism where learning and habits occur. Unfortunately, when this occurrence is not natural, it can lead to neurodevelopmental disorders.

Now, why do these changes occur? There is a trait of the human brain that makes it unique and different from other organs: "Neuroplasticity," which simply means that the brain is "plastic" or adaptable by nature. It is constantly changing and adapting to your lifestyle and behavior. Due to neuroplasticity, we are continually learning or creating new habits. However, it also allows bad habits like substance abuse, turn into dependence, creating lasting effects in the brain, like reducing a considerable number of synapses or "grey matter" in the brain. It also makes falling into old habits easier. Because a solid synaptic connection is already there when practice is old, the impulse to go down the same path is stronger. It's simply easier for the brain.

The reward mechanism, also called the NAc-VTA Circuitry, exuberates all addictions. Understanding how it works will shed light on many if not all of an addicted person's behavior. In the brain, we have a part named the striatum. Also called the nucleus accumbens (NAc), it is the part that controls motivation or is responsible for pursuing rewards. You see, every movement of human beings is influenced by motivation or the urge to go after something they want. We hardly have any natural subconscious trigger-based reactions, as you see on insects or non-mammals. For example, when you lift your hand, it is to reach for something. We, as mammals, act by pursuing goals. What is the cause of pursuing that goal? Reward, of course! The promise of reward makes us want to do things.

The brain's way of rewarding is by secreting a dose of dopamine that induces a feeling of pleasure. Dopamine is released from a part named the ventral tegmental area (VTA) of the midbrain. Apart from creating the sense of pleasure, among many dopamine functions is making sure you learn how to create that pleasure again. After the VTA releases dopamine, it in turn activates the striatum amygdala, which mediates emotions and remembers whether a particular environmental cue was pleasurable or not. The same happens to the hippocampus, which controls memory, and several prefrontal cortex regions responsible for thinking and choice-making. So, when you do something (take drugs, shop, sex) for the first time, it feels good, and dopamine is released. The released dopamine goes to the striatum, amygdala, and prefrontal cortex, which recognizes the behavior or condition as pleasurable and remembers it. So, next time the opportunity arises to do the same thing, one desires to do it.

# 6

# STAGES OF ADDICTION

Scientists have suggested different addiction stages. The most accepted and recent one is the three stages of addiction mentioned in the Surgeon General's Report.

- Binge and intoxication,
- Withdrawal and negative affect, and
- Preoccupation and anticipation (or craving).

The goal and reward system is how we learned from childhood and did since creation. Are you hungry and see something that resembles food? The goal the brain has set is to eat it because you have experienced eating food when hungry. Do you love the food? If yes, your brain gives you a dopamine rush as a reward. As a result, you know now that eating that particular food makes you feel good; you "learn" a new thing. So, next time you see that food, you get an urge to eat it. Kids love to eat candy because sugar increases dopamine levels, so the brain has "learned" that sugary treats are good.

## BINGE AND INTOXICATION

This first stage is when the substance starts to affect the user's brain. So, it starts activating reward regions with the secretion of dopamine each time it is used. As the dopamine receptors are activated repeatedly, associative learning or conditioning is triggered. This is a type of Pavlovian conditioning. If the term is unfamiliar to you, it simply means training or conditioning the brain to respond a certain way when facing a set of stimuli.

When the brain experiences the same reward after encountering the same environmental conditions, it associates it with the environment. It stimulates the rewarding center by only facing the surroundings, even without the substances. Let me give an example in layman's terms. After a person takes drugs for a while, his brain relates the environment he is in (friends that he uses with, place, or even the emotion which leads to taking them) and the rush of dopamine he gets after taking them together. So, each time he is in that environment, he gets a rush of dopamine, thus creating a craving for the substance. This type of learning is actually not uncommon with other habits as well. We seek food and sleep through the exact same rewarding mechanism.

However, when it comes to most types of addictions, there is no limit.

Now, since rewards also reinforce goal-seeking behavior, the dorsal striatum (situated close to the ventral striatum) also gets involved when a person uses for a long time. The ventral striatum gets less excited with continual use, and the dorsal striatum becomes the focus of dopamine-induced excitation. At this stage, the person becomes an addict in all senses of the word. See, the dorsal striatum creates compulsive behavior; so, the person no longer needs to be in the presence of an environmental cue; rather, he feels the need to get high all on his own. And this compulsion is powerful and defies reason. The frenzy we often see in addicts is the result of it.

There are several explanations for why it happens. After a person abuses substances for a long time, the dopamine produced in their brain loses its potency at a cellular level. Actual brain scans of addicts show marked reductions in D2 dopamine receptors and dopamine release in the striatum in long-term addicted subjects. So not only is there a reduced amount of dopamine release, but there is also a smaller number of receptors to create the "feel good" experience. So, this causes a problem in their day-to-day lives. The brain now produces and releases a lesser amount of dopamine naturally; the usual stuff that used to produce dopamine, like eating good food, talking to a friend, playing games, etc., may not create any dopamine. Or, even if they generate some dopamine, the resulting feeling is very low due to the low number of receptors, So, he loses interest in these things. You may have noticed these changes in your son's behavior as he passed this stage of addiction. The sudden and unexplained disinterest in school, throwing away or pawning his favorite sneakers, or not enjoying his meals can all be explained as due to the lack of dopamine and dopamine receptors.

Furthermore, this lack makes him feel anxious, depressed, or withdrawn. It is easy to understand if you think about it. Ordinary things that we do every day keep us on a healthy, low amount of dopamine flow. And with it, we feel normal and stable. Now, if that were suddenly taken away, we would not feel normal. Our brain would tell us that something is very wrong. That is what addicts feel when they are sober; at this point, they feel the need to go to their source, which creates some sense of control, stability, or comfort to feel "normal." They already have some damage to their brains with only a small amount of dopamine and too few receptors. At this point, what all drugs do for them now is fire those few receptors and give them the same level of "high" or "good" an average person feels when eating a delicious meal. (So, not an actual high, but just a good feeling.) At this stage of addiction, even a moderate dose of substances makes an addict feel only slightly good but does not induce euphoria.

## WITHDRAWAL AND NEGATIVE AFFECT

This effect explains a couple of behaviors of addicts. This "low" an addicted person feels is why when they are taken off the substance forcibly after using too long, they often experience severe withdrawal symptoms, become depressed, and may contemplate suicide. Substance abuse has long been connected to suicide, and most studies conclude that the depression, anger, frustration, and oftentimes mental illness a substance-dependent person experiences fuel their suicidal thoughts.

The part of the brain that controls, fear, anxiety, and all the bad feelings is the amygdala. It also assesses whether some experience feels "good" or "bad." So, as we discussed before, dopamine becomes very low when a long-term addicted person is sober. At this stage, the amygdala reacts aggressively because it assumes he is in a stressful condition (due to the lower-than-average dopamine level). So, the extended amygdala creates feelings like anxiety, pain, unease, and even fear. Withdrawal symptoms can be severe, sometimes fatal, for example, in opioid addiction or for someone with a history of cardiac issues or seizures. Sometimes, when he is on drugs long enough, he takes more to avoid withdrawal symptoms. At this stage, a teen or young adult may get violent or furious if anyone comes between him and his addiction. In rehab, the doctors use medications that act the same way as drugs but without tolerance and dependency effects. These allow a person's brain to detox without going through painful episodes of withdrawal.

## PREOCCUPATION AND ANTICIPATION

But it still doesn't explain the "frenzy," right? There are some other effects of long-term drug abuse I haven't explained yet. And it is the last and 3rd stage of addiction. It is called the Preoccupation/Anticipation Stage. When a person is addicted long enough, the brain's prefrontal area that controls thinking, decision-making, managing time, organizing thoughts and activities, prioritizing tasks, and regulating actions, emotions, and impulses are affected. This area becomes less and less active. The impulses begin to take over, which explains why a substance abuser often performs poorly at work, gets terrible grades, and cannot make rational decisions even on simple matters. The damage to this area can last a long time, so much so that even after prolonged abstinence, he may relapse to old habits as his ability to inhibit impulses is impaired.

Another factor is also important to note. With the reductions in D2 DA receptors in the striatum, there is a reduction of the orbitofrontal cortex (OFC) activity. The OFC is the region involved with salience attribution, motivation, and compulsive behaviors. There is also a reduction of activity in the cingulate gyrus (CG), the part involved with inhibitory control and impulsivity. As a result, when sober, these areas of the addict's brain have less activity. But when he uses substances, they start working. Hence, he feels high motivation and compulsion to keep the habit. This compulsion to use substances overrides any competing cognitive-based tendencies or common sense to avoid it. These two areas (CG and OFC) are also involved with inhibitory control. So, any inhibitions he may have felt beforehand regarding using are gone. There is no rational thought, only the need to use.

There is a set of behavior that substance abusers usually express at this stage. These include lack of remorse, continually lying to parents, friends, or teachers, manipulating for money, stealing, dealing, and all kinds of risky behaviors. They also start being highly secretive, always on guard, and careful about what they say or do. You may have noticed behavior changes, new friends, mysterious disappearances, missed school, unfinished homework, failing grades, excuses, narcissistic and antisocial personalities, and the list goes on.

You see, if your son has been using for a long time, it becomes hard for him to feel anything else too strongly. The need for substance takes over other rational behavior and feelings. He gets triggered easily; social isolation and disinterest in school events or social gatherings is typical addict behavior. It may seem like an expected teen growth spurt, but in reality, he has lost the control he was seeking. The emotional void he was trying to fill is still a gaping hole. Soon he hates everyone and everything, avoids family, stays stuck in his room, skips family gatherings, spends the holidays with unfamiliar "friends." Not to mention avoiding conversations and confrontations. The mom becomes the enemy to him due to the reaction and attempts to come between him and his perceived solution and to help him gets difficult. In his brain, he always seeks to justify his actions with the belief that the behavior is beneficial or necessary. He is then said to be in denial and rejects most help. At this stage, a mom has to devise new strategies to approach the issue.

# 7

# OTHER ADDICTIONS

W e mentioned that there are many types of addictions, and they follow the same brain development and mechanism. The outward symptoms are often the same, but the compulsion and withdrawals are less severe in non-substance addiction. Although these addictions don't raise as much alarm as drug and alcohol addictions, any substance abuse is unhealthy and damaging to a person's health, life, and relationships. Have you ever been an addict? Let's find out...

## INTERNET AND PHONE ADDICTIONS

According to common sense media, about 78 percent of teens spend an average of 7 hours and 22 minutes on their phones daily, excluding the screen time spent on school and homework. This number is higher now, especially after the COVID19 pandemic. Young people wake up at night to check their phones or respond to a message. Psychiatrists call obsessive internet scrolling problematic as they interfere with regular life routines affecting the quality of life. Cell phone addiction can be so severe that teens may be unable to focus without phones, and their attention span becomes short and fragile.

## PORN AND SEX ADDICTIONS

Interest and attraction towards the opposite sex are part of growing up. But, becoming addicted to it is entirely different and can harm normal sexual development and relationships. Sex-addicted people and those who watch porn often may have multiple partners, thereby exposing themselves to STDs, hepatitis, AIDS, etc. They do not see the act as an expression of love. While the act may produce some euphoria, the addict is left cold and empty as the act is devoid of emotion and connection, yet he still seeks the habit again and again.

## FOOD ADDICTIONS

Eating disorders can develop as a means of coping or seeking control in a person who has experienced adversity, trauma, or tragedy in childhood. One type of disorder is food addiction in teens, especially American teens, which is on the rise. The high availability of junk food, sugary treats, and TV dinners are just too many addictive options. They seek food for comfort, and the addict craves the food and can barely think of anything else. So, they indulge, overeat, snack constantly, or binge eat and end up feeling worse afterwards, especially if they are obese or their health is threatened, but they cannot stop.

## WORK ADDICTIONS

Workaholics will often work compulsively. They may not necessarily love what they do, but in an attempt to fill an underlying psychological need, they avoid others, work late hours, take their work home, travel often, or justify spending for work. Vacations are a waste of time to them, and they will be found filling this time with work instead of spending time with family. While being motivated towards success is commendable, work addiction actually destroys relationships, leads to burnout, exhaustion, mood swings, and poor time management. A workaholic will mention how much his company needs him to work overtime, justifying neglect of his family and health.

## GAMING ADDICTIONS

Apart from the compulsion of gaming, spending money on new video games, and playing at all hours, gaming hinders physical health, schoolwork, social life, and relationships. It is addictive and encourages laziness, tardiness, and obesity common among young video game players.

## SHOPPING ADDICTIONS

Another compulsive habit involves buying on impulse, often leading to financial distress. Shopaholics usually tend to overbuy, shop for things they never use or need. They experience a high while shopping and showing off to friends and family but quickly lose interest and go off seeking more things to buy. The term "retail therapy" is associated with shopaholics because they shop with the sole purpose of lifting their mood or relieving stress. A shopaholic will explain how much he needs that new pair of sneakers regardless of whether he wears it or not.

## GAMBLING ADDICTIONS

Gambling like drugs is very gripping. Gamblers get high on the uncertainty and the adrenaline they feel when gambling. They take significant risks and often exchange something valuable, like betting a whole month's income, hoping to get something of greater value. The compulsion does not cease despite losing repeatedly.

Your son may not be addicted to all or any of the above. No matter which addiction though, the good news is that it's all reversible. It is a challenging process and certainly not possible without having a good grasp of what an addict is going through. Once you understand and empathize, it is possible to feel his pain, struggle, and guilt. Addicts will often pretend to be confident and in control of themselves, but it's a facade. They even lie to themselves, while they are actually just confused and scared, and their brain cannot function optimally. In this confusing and painful condition, what an addict needs is a friend, a guide, a sympathetic person; quite simply, he needs you.

# STEP# 2

## CONNECTING ADDICTIONS TO TRAUMA

# 8

# CHOICE OR GENETIC?

In the previous chapters, we discussed addiction in depth. We examined and dissected the rarely understood yet highly prevalent condition from various angles, trying to understand it better. I hope that as you understood addiction more deeply with each paragraph, you were also developing an understanding of your son's struggles and history. As we know now, addiction is not the problem, just the sign that something has been wrong all along. Hidden beneath the surface are years of misunderstood emotions and trauma, which lead to insufferable pain.

My church's missionary team served food to the homeless most of them addicts, I sympathized with their plight, but I never thought much about their backgrounds, their moms, and the reasons behind their addictions until it happened to me. I hope, like me, your mind has shifted, and you have developed more compassion and empathy for not only your son but other users too. I know my perception changed, and now I view all addicts differently. I wonder about them and how their moms must feel.

As we seek to understand the roots of addictions more deeply, we must eliminate certain misconceptions while identifying the possible causes. The most common one being that it's a choice. Moms often have this idea that their son may have chosen addiction over them, their family, school, sports, hobbies, career, job, or as an act of rebellion, irresponsibility, or a 'don't care attitude.' You will often hear it from other parents and guardians as well. A mom will compare before and after pictures of her son and loudly wonder, "Why did he choose heroin? "Of all the habits to pick, why did my precious son choose this?" Haven't I given him enough love? Did he stop to think of his poor mother just once? Doesn't he know what this does to his family? This thought pattern is heartbreaking and often the force that pulls families apart.

We, the society, always portray addiction as a failure in life's choices. A choice someone consciously made, a lapse of judgment, a lack of morale, or genetic disease. When a person is addicted, we automatically assume that he somehow is destined to fail at becoming a respectable member of society. Some experts claim that once an addict, always an addict, labeling the person vulnerable to spiraling right back at the whiff of a drink or drug.

If addictive behaviors were a choice, one would decide to quit anytime, but if seen as a response to adversity or emotional deprivation in childhood, moms would understand why more intervention is required.

If addiction is not a disease or an active choice, what could it be? The debate is still out there whether addiction is genetic. This misconception derives from the fact that children who come from families of addicts often develop addiction as well. While this may be factual, it is not due to genetic makeup. Genes are the codes or bricks that make our bodies. If we were a book, genes would be the chapters. As you can imagine, genes control quite a bit of a person's characteristics. For example, genes control whether they will have green eyes or blue eyes or whether they will be tall or short. As genes "code" for all body structures and functions, the alterations or mistakes in gene "coding" result in malfunctions or disease. Understand that illnesses are generally not due to genetic mishaps, but some families are predisposed to certain conditions, and some experts attribute this to genetics.

Early experiences in life affect genetic expressions, but the gene must exist in the first place! When experts talk about environmental factors affecting genes, they often mean that not having the ideal environment can "turn off" genes. For example, if a person's gene says he is to be tall and he gets malnourished or abused in childhood, his "tall gene" is inactivated. People wrongly assume that there is a gene for every trait a person has. Behavioral characteristics are mostly not "coded" by genes. For example, whether a person will be a "gambler" or be "compassionate" is not written by genes. It is developed as a trait by conscious decisions, subconscious mind, and experiences in life or environment. Addiction, therefore, is not a genetic phenomenon either, even though it is often passed on through generations.

# 9

# GENERATIONAL CYCLE

The correlation between addicts and the presence of abusive or neglectful parents, grandparents, or other caretakers who themselves may have been addicts (due to their own traumatic experiences) is notable. When several researchers first pointed out this relation, it became clear that the addiction cycle often passed on in families had some more predisposed than others. In actuality, the correlation is due to the adversity the children go through at the hands of mentally ill, addicted, absent, abusive, or unhappy caretakers. Some children are more resilient, and others are more sensitive, so they all may turn out differently. Some become addicts; others don't, others develop chronic illnesses, and some, despite traumatic experiences, turn out okay, seemingly unaffected.

It is essential to understand that not everything a child goes through is necessarily considered traumatic by adults. A child may grow up with emotionally absent parents, provided with every physical comfort, but deprived of emotional support. Here the parents fail to respond to their child's feelings, and when they grow up, they unconsciously do this same thing to their children since it is normal for them. Consequently, they may develop addictions; and the cycle continues.

It can be challenging to connect the signs, even as an adult. Children do not have the capacity or composure to express themselves verbally or clearly. When agitated, they show agitation through crying, fussing, acting out (remember the terrible twos?), or isolation (in teens). They naturally have a narrower, biased, narcissistic view of the world, focusing primarily on themselves. So, when an adult ignores, punishes, or is neglectful or hurtful, they assume it is their fault and since this kind of treatment is traumatic and they do not understand the emotional turmoil they experience, the trauma remains in the body and affects the mind. A child cannot differentiate between cues and actions and will believe that whatever negativity he faces is deserved. It is another reason they never come to an adult with these emotional concerns because they don't understand them either.

Any child can experience trauma, and everyone's level of what would be considered a traumatic experience is different and affects everyone differently. Besides addiction, some develop chronic diseases, respiratory illnesses like asthma, skin conditions like eczema, or even obesity. Others develop depression, anxiety, ADD, ADHD, and other mental issues.

The cycle continues when a person dealing with these issues becomes a parent. She may not offer a healthy environment for her children. She may unknowingly abuse without realizing the long-term effects of such abuse. If a mom cannot recognize some factors as childhood adversity, how does she know how it affects her children? She doesn't!

According to Dr. Nadine Burke, one of the greatest advocates for using the Adverse Childhood Experiences score test to identify ACE score, having a "reliable adult to go to" can lessen the impact of adverse childhood. As the children of the struggling parents may not have any stable environment or guardian, they often suffer the trauma alone. These children grow up and raise their own but struggle with the effect of their childhood adversity and unwilfully hurt their children, and the cycle continues.

# 10

# CHILDHOOD TRAUMA AND ENVIRONMENT

In his research regarding mental conditions like OCD and PTSD and his book "Traumatic stress," Dr. Bessel van der Kolk MD, psychiatrist, educator, researcher, and author, mentions a phenomenon named Traumatic Reminders. He calls them external and internal cues specific to the person's traumatic experiences. So, it can be anything related to the traumatic experience; a person, loud voices, a place, smell, or even some gesture like picking up a baseball bat. These traumatic reminders are the cues that trigger post-traumatic stress reactions.

Unanticipated traumatic reminders can evoke a sense of unpreparedness that exacerbates the fear of recurrence. Suddenly facing some environmental reminder of the trauma can induce fear of facing the trauma again. Although you know logically that cannot happen, you still feel fear and uneasiness.

That is the nature of trauma. In the mind of most people, it is not a detailed, single memory, rather many small fragments of the events. People often cannot recall everything that happened. Whether a single event or a string of events happening for years, these memories are often tied together with emotions and environmental cues. When one faces the traumatic reminder, one may have illogical reactions to it. The responses vary from slight discomfort to a strong sense of fear, panic attacks, and even physical pain, often leading to withdrawal, fear of confrontations, lashing out, or seeking control in risky behavior.

Envision it like this, if you had gotten any kind of severe injury to one of your limbs when you were young, and even it had healed, the damage would still cause a limiting effect on your movements. There may be scarring and stunted growth, the limb moving differently. Our brain is like that. When you suffer a traumatic event, the damage it does to the brain is not easily identified or reversible. Even if the physical pain of the trauma goes away, there will always be some ghost of the initial injury left. As injury to the mind is not visible like injury to the body, the wound never heals and continues to fester and eventually become difficult to contain without some sort of temporary relief.

Dr. Bessel says that research proves that it is almost impossible to be a drug addict without having a prior history of childhood trauma. Therefore, substance abuse in teens and young adults usually starts as a way of coping with the mental trauma they may have experienced in the past as babies or are going through currently. Dr. Gabor Maté, on the other hand, says,

*"Addictions arise from thwarted love, from our thwarted ability to love children the way they need to be loved, from our thwarted ability to love ourselves and one another in the ways we all need."*

— DR. GABOR MATÉ

It may not seem like much to an adult, but to a child, most environmental experiences are traumatic,

Children develop different personalities, which can become maladjusted by their growth environment and relationships. These can be exhibited in mental or emotional health issues. A happy, talkative boy may suddenly become closed and withdrawn. I can say for sure that my son, who used to be a chatterbox, became so closed that getting information from him felt like pulling teeth. I sensed it was because he perceived my disappointment or a response to my not understanding his behavior. That, and the guilt and shame of what he had become and was putting himself through.

It is hard to believe, but these boys never choose to become addicts. Every recovered addict I have listened to talks with deep regret about the guilt, shame, and pain he experienced or caused his family. The majority actively using, desire to quit, but most don't find a better or safer alternative.

There is almost always a reason around the environment or relationships when they start abusing substances. Often, the reason is psychological, hidden from the sufferer but seen in uncontrollable behavior or habits. This person is searching for control, an attempt to fill a void, shield himself from emotional pain, or a desire to fit in. He may have unknowingly gone through a traumatic or long-forgotten experience, but the mental anguish still lives on, affecting behaviors and decision-making processes.

Addiction is seldom presented as what it is, a sign of internal struggle and suffering. And instead of offering addicts compassion and love, these kids are generally met with hostility, criticism, judgment, and mistrust. Roy (our boy in chapter 1) felt ridiculed for substance use. The feeling of disdain and self-loathing because of the social portrayal of addicts made him more drawn to substances. His inability to quit was as aggravating to himself as it was to his mom.

A teen or young adult starts risky behaviors to enjoy a sense of control, avoid emotional or physical pain, feel happy, experience a sense of belonging, or escape reality.

An adverse experience in the past could be triggered by a recent incident that brings unpleasant memories that need to be avoided. After a while, in addition to the suffering he was already facing, the addict starts to experience physical, emotional, and social alienation, magnifying the suffering. When actively using, he is ashamed to face his parents, teachers, or friends' disappointments. So, he attempts to hide his problem from everyone, all the while struggling to stay afloat. The loved ones, the ones who he wishes would understand, accuse, judge, and maybe worse, alienate the user. Most substance abusers experience this sense of acute isolation, helplessness, unhappiness, and anger toward themselves and the world around them and hope to find solace in their addiction. Seeking help seems complicated, and they are said to be in denial.

Teens with family and personal histories may even feel that succumbing to addiction is inevitable. So, the question to ask yourself as a mom is not "why is my son an addict?" instead, ask, "What happened to my baby? Why is my son in pain?" Find the answer to that, and you will also find the key to helping him. Your job as a parent is to inform yourself about all the aspects of addiction and trauma, be the strength he needs, and be at peace with yourself. Only through empathy can healing begin.

# TRAUMATIC EXPERIENCES

Some environmental factors that could lead to trauma and ultimately to addiction include emotional and physical abuse. It can be intentional or unintentional, but it is often perpetrated by people who have been abused, experienced adversity in childhood, or had a mental illness. Abuse includes misfortunes that a child has no control over yet are traumatic.

Yelling and screaming do not have to be directed at the child. Just being in an environment where they witness fights or anger is traumatic enough; even the ones adults feel "rightful." One of the ACEs test questions (which we shall discuss shortly) is whether the child was present when others physically or verbally abused an adult. Parents may be in the next room yelling, and this scares the children. The older child may naturally fall into the role of the protector of the other siblings, especially if there is violence involved. But who gets to protect him? Maybe no one. He may turn out seemingly responsible and often withdrawn as he learns to repress his feelings, then he becomes a teen and seeks emotional stability in substances. Sometimes he doesn't but may develop an introverted personality with uncontrollable outbursts of anger. This can be confusing to others if they do not realize that he has gone through traumatic experiences.

In abuse, injury or harm is inflicted on a vulnerable minor who cannot protect himself. These forms of abuse have long-term emotional effects.

## SEXUAL ABUSE

Most of these cases go unreported, and while more girls than boys are sexually abused before the age of 16, substance abuse is used to cope with the trauma by both sexes. Such abused children are at a higher risk of substance abuse than those who experience other adversities. When it happens at a very young age, a child may not understand what happened, but he is affected psychologically and may develop perplexing issues like obesity. Sometimes, kids who may be close to their moms hide traumatic events like sexual abuse because they believe they are to blame. Or they do not recognize it as abuse if it includes touching or an adult indecently exposing himself in front of the child.

## NEGLECT

Neglect happens when a child is deprived of the physical or emotional interaction he needs from moms or caregivers. Infants and babies specifically need to be held, nurtured, and cherished. Even if caregivers like nannies are present, children often feel the absence of parents acutely. Other nannies may be negligent, and when these kids are sent to daycare, then left to sleep alone every night, they lose out on the touch they so crave. Emotional neglect from moms is not intentional. Most of the time, the moms themselves are not aware they are neglecting their children. They may have been deprived as children or currently facing some issues in their lives, like losing a parent, their job, demanding jobs, moving, divorce, separation, or even the presence of many children preventing them from giving adequate time and attention to some kids. For a sensitive child, this apparently negligible amount of negligence can be traumatic.

## ABANDONMENT

It can be due to the early death of one or both parents, loss of family, living in an orphanage, foster care system, divorce of parents, or a mother who cannot care for her child, leaving him with relatives or strangers.

A mom who experienced adversity as a child or an addict can abandon her son, unable to provide the emotional support he needs. He may grow up feeling unwanted, and as a teen or young adult boy, his addicted friends may be the ones who fill this need and emotional gap.

## EXTREME PUNISHMENTS

Disciplining a child is expected of every mom, but some forms could be exceedingly damaging to his mental, physical, and emotional health. Time out or the silent treatment teaches him that he has lost the right to "exist" if he does something wrong. He also views love as conditional, only given when he is 'good.'

Beatings, spanking, yelling are other unnecessary punishments. There is a common phrase, "spare the rod and spoil the child."

> *"He that spareth his rod hates his son: but he that loveth him chasteneth him betimes."*
>
> — PROVERBS 13:24

Moms often used this saying out of context, and they would brutally beat up their children in the name of love. It was customary to whip a child as young as two years old to discipline him. But what moms were not taught was to seek to understand why he was misbehaving or acting out in the first place. In this situation, it was hard for him to understand the reason for the punishment. Generally, children who are beaten or spanked get worse, not better.

Hopefully, moms no longer hit their kids. Spanking is unnecessary when they are redirected with love while other more humane methods of discipline are used. A child should especially never be disciplined in anger. It is hard to convince your son that spanking, which causes pain and low self-esteem, is an act of love.

Talking to your boy calmly without any irritation and redirecting him to do something more productive is way more effective. There is almost always a reason why children act the way they do, and most behaviors are just ways kids try to communicate a need. This applies to teens' and young adults' behaviors as well.

## OVER STRICTNESS

According to research, most people believe that strict parenting produces better-behaved children. However, research on discipline consistently shows that strict, or authoritarian, child-rearing produces kids with lower self-esteem who behave worse than other children – and thus are punished more! Strict parenting causes behavioral issues in childhood and later in life.

As teenagers and young adults, boys raised with a strict parenting style tend to be angrier and more rebellious; they don't learn how to self-regulate; they learn to lie more, obey out of fear, and bully others. They do not think for themselves and may not question authority when they should later in life. They are less likely to accept responsibility for their actions, are more likely to follow the peer group, and avoid responsibility as they are simply "following orders."

Authoritarian parenting teaches children that a part of themselves is unacceptable. Their parents aren't there to help them learn to cope with and manage the complex feelings that drive them to act out. They are left alone, trying to figure out how to overcome impulses, and can easily grow to abuse substances.

## MOLLYCODDLING

All moms desire to protect their sons, and they should. But boys must not be overprotected and must learn about consequences at an early age. For example, he needs to know to amble because he can fall, and a mom does not need to hover over him to make sure he does not fall. The only way he can learn is by falling.

Being too permissive is also detrimental as it teaches him that all his desires must be granted, even harmful ones, like if he decides to sleep late watching TV. Or that he can get whatever he wants at the expense of others. He must learn that disappointments are a part of life, that he cannot always get the phone he wants. Permissiveness affects your son's development and ability to make decisions. He never develops self-discipline and control and is said to be 'spoilt.' A mom may grant this freedom because she wants to ensure his well-being or not annoy him, but instead, she loses control while he loses his individuality, unable to cope independently. When he turns into an addict, this loss of control by the mum may aggravate the situation as he is no longer controllable, yet he does not have the coping skills to survive without the security of his home.

Going through this list may make you emotional and guilty. I know I was. After all, I am guilty of one or two in the list. The purpose of listing this is not to portray you as a bad or negligent mother or to point fingers at your method of upbringing, far from it. Like I stated earlier, all and every mother, even the abusive ones, do their best when raising their sons, and abusing them is a response to their traumas. We gathered that addiction is more than meets the eye; it signifies that your boy needs your help, not that he is selfish or rebellious.

The list mentioned above is not conclusive and not all that sparks addiction in later life. As a mom, you probably cannot think of a single reason why your son developed the habit. Where despite having loving, doting parents, he still became vulnerable to substances. But it is futile to believe that there is such a thing as perfection where a family has never experienced trauma. Traumatic experiences sometimes happen without the parent's knowledge, and the child never speaks of it because he cannot connect the implications or was too young to know that they had happened.

A rift in the family unit may also cause trauma, driving your son to desert the home and spend time with questionable friends. And this is something I can relate to; I relocated and left my son under the care of relatives just after he became a teenager. Even after several attempts, many years passed, and we were still not reunited. I believe this rift greatly impacted him, seeing we were close before that. Suddenly he had no authoritative figure in his life, felt unloved and unwanted, and he soon preferred the company of his friends to my family. His constant refusal to spend time with them was a huge red flag that I missed.

# TRAUMATIC FLASHBACKS

I n her book Prisoners of Childhood, Alice Miller said, and I quote,

*"The truth about our childhood is stored in our bodies and lives in the depths of our souls. And although we can repress it, we can never alter it. Our intellect can be deceived, our feelings can be numbed and manipulated, our perceptions shamed and confused, our bodies tricked with medication, but our soul never forgets. And because we are one, one whole soul in one body, someday our body will present its bill."*

— ALICE MILLER

In modern medicine, the root cause of illnesses is largely ignored. Treatments are based on the symptoms one is experiencing, not on adversities that could have happened years before. The trauma event may not have been traumatic as we regard trauma, but the body remembers it as such, and this cause to effect is always overlooked.

They are all around us, many moms hurting and crying for their sons who started abusing substances at the tender age of 12- 14 years. They do not know how it started and certainly don't know how to end it. They have struggled for years, battling with the roller coaster ride without a solution in sight.

And I was having such a conversation with Linda.

Linda asked for prayers because she had found a treatment center in a different state, and her son Greg had agreed to get help. It was his fifth trip to rehab; he had relapsed all four times, had overdosed at least twice, and had been in jail for drunk driving once. Linda told me she cried almost every night; she was tired, troubled, and unsure this time would be any better. Her other children seemed okay and happy. Except for the 27-year-old son, it would otherwise be labeled a happy home.

She got talking about her other family; her parents argued often, and she was always scared of her father. Her husband used to smoke weed and drink during the first years of their marriage. Greg was born around this time, the marriage was difficult initially because her husband was as domineering as her father was, and she always felt scared, unheard, and out of control. She admitted that Greg could have been affected by their unstable years of marriage, but she had no idea how to help except pray for a miracle. Although her husband had mellowed and no longer abused substances, her son was causing her so much anguish that she had a constant sense of impending doom. For so long, she had hoped things would turn around.

Like any mom, your intuition never lies to you, even when you try to rationalize what is not evident. Things may seem okay on the surface, and nobody else may see it when you try to share your unease.

It took a while before Linda acknowledged that her son was an addict. She had seen the red flags, yet she had trouble confronting this issue and was afraid her husband would abandon her. As we spoke and she reflected on all her fears, the signs she had missed, everything started to make sense.

I felt like I understood Linda. It is highly probable she had been tuning out her pain, panic, and anxiety for years, as a child, then as a wife and mother. Where else could the fear of confrontation and abandonment be rooted? Was it not trauma she experienced as a child?

Trauma is like a tissue wound, and it heals but always leaves a scar. It is almost always impossible to be completely free of the experiences we had in our earlier life. Memories of those experiences come at us at unexpected times and suddenly. Sometimes they don't come as memories rather as reactions that shape our personalities.

When raising him, a mom may think that her son has a strange personality, but he may just be reacting to an experience, either by getting distressed, crying a lot, disinterested in play, avoiding eye contact, clinginess, not showing feelings, or having a scared look. Understandably, mothers must work or go to school. So being aware that these traumas can be soothed by being fully present, having close hugs, and spending quality time with her son when she gets home is very important.

A mom, more than the dad, has a more significant responsibility for influencing the son's disposition and character because she is the one who carries the baby in her womb and spends most of the time with him growing up. The habits of the mom can affect the unborn or infant child either positively or negatively. She could be stressed, unstable, unhappy, or loving, happy, and stress-free; her son can bear these traits. Either way, moms keenly feel the effects of their son's pain and exhaust themselves more when trying to help.

Psychiatrists often stress how much effect a person's previous experiences, especially childhood experiences, have on adult life. They shape our subconscious without any of us realizing it. Some of it is very apparent and easy to notice, and you will see it in yourself or the people around you. For example, some people may fear water or heights because they had a bad experience as children and were left with a negative imprint regarding these concepts. Some, however, are difficult to spot, even by the person experiencing them.

Take Linda's experience, for example. She is successful, married, and with a beautiful family. Her son is in serious trouble, but she still feels scared of abandonment and confrontations and cannot express her feelings. Curiously, she is not aware of how problematic this could be. For Linda, the adverse childhood environment caused anxiety, fear, and even obsessive fear of confrontations and uncomfortable situations. She believed that she needed to be docile to be accepted, and unknowingly, her experiences modeled her marriage and family life.

As a reminder or cue that we associate with our trauma can induce flashbacks, the time of the actual traumatic event matters. The younger a child, the more its effect on the brain (remember in the last chapters we talked about nerve receptor formation?) Even if you have moved from the environment or overcame your fear and hatred or whatever emotion those traumatic events induced, the shadow still lurks. In a sense, trauma is like an invisible demon that refuses to give up. Why did I call it invisible? Well, the traumatic event or events one had to suffer through are stark, visible events in their lives, but the trauma is not always obvious.

Some people do not get panic attacks or fear when facing a traumatic reminder; they feel no discernible emotional changes even when facing major environmental cues like place or person. However, they are not free of the trauma, and instead, it has a more prominent control over them expressed through their behaviors and lifestyle choices. You notice that some abuse substances, some become meek and quiet, some avoid confrontation, and some crave affection, attention, or validation. All these traits are subtle changes we can see but hardly suspect as a byproduct of traumatic experiences.

Arguably, we are all somewhat controlled by our pasts. According to research, our subconscious mind controls much of what we do on a day-to-day basis. Thus, the condition of the subconscious mind is directly proportional to the behaviors and actions of a person. These actions can be voluntary or involuntary. Voluntary actions include speaking or not speaking, going somewhere or not going, moving to defend yourself, or not doing something, etc. Understand that these decisions usually come from the involuntary subconscious, but the action itself is voluntary. Meaning, when you agree to go to a pub with your friend, you may or may not be influenced by the subconscious mind to make that decision, but the actual going part (moving your legs) is voluntary. Involuntary actions are like muscle twitching or flinching. People often do it without realizing they are doing it. Someone may flinch when they hear a loud voice; the inducer is mostly the subconscious mind. So even when we believe we are taking a decision voluntarily, freely, or willingly, it often comes from unconscious emotional drives or subliminal beliefs. In other words, we are not as in control as we like to think we are.

Freedom, or free will, is quite challenging to achieve if you are unaware of what is happening.

In an interview, addiction expert, Gabor Maté said,

---

*"It's a subtle thing, freedom. It takes effort; it takes attention and focus not to act something like an automaton. Although we do have freedom, we exercise it only when we strive for awareness, when we are conscious not just of the content of the mind but also of the mind itself as a process."*

— GABOR MATÉ

---

The truth is we are all somehow controlled by our experiences and expectations. When we are born, we have only basic needs and feelings. We feel hunger and pain. Other emotions come later, sculpted by the environment around us. It is quite a standard basis of brain development in children. Our emotional reactions and behaviors are molded after the environment of our upbringing. For example, a child raised in a family that emphasizes compassion is likely to show behaviors that reflect that as an adult. Still, if he wanted to, he could choose not to show compassion. It would be based on his choices, one that he could freely make without much effort.

However, the difference in abused children is that the negativity they grew up in locks some emotions and behaviors in a set pattern. They can and do function like any other people, except for some facets of social and personal life where they feel stuck. For example, someone raised in a violent environment may automatically avoid violent confrontations as a defense mechanism to avoid becoming the victim. Alternatively, he may turn violent to maintain control. Someone who grew up without hugs or physical contact will seek physical affection in any form as an adult or not associate an intimate act like sex with love and emotion. These actions or sets of actions are controlled by brain mechanisms cataloged by childhood events and trauma.

According to Dr. Schwartz, M.D psychiatrist, researcher, and his team, it is difficult to break these patterns without awareness and deliberate counter actions. Even then, it all depends on how healthy your conscious brain is. In simpler terms, the strength of the conscious decision-making part of a person's brain determines how much actual control they have over their actions and behavior. Unfortunately, people who suffered trauma in early childhood tend to malfunction that part of the brain. Thus, unbeknownst to them, they are often not in total control of their actions.

# 13

# MY EXPERIENCES

Talking to Linda and hearing her fears of confrontations, rejection and abandonment made me think about my past. Am I not living in a similar emotional state as she is?

Or have I healed my wounds and moved on? In a way, Linda and I were like kindred spirits. When I reflected on my past, I could see some commonalities. Her father and mine? Different in several ways but alike in the way they affected us. Her father had anger issues, was known to get into fits of rage, and often threatened to kick her and her mom from home. They often ran away to avoid his furious outbursts but always returned as her mother had no way of supporting them. Then her mom died when she was just a teen.

My reflections brought some unresolved issues to the surface. See, I do not remember much before age five, it would almost be impossible to remember what happened to you before that age, but I do remember that my mother, who was constantly stressed, went to live in the country when I was around nine years old. I visited her during school breaks, as I grew up with my dad, a high-functioning alcoholic, back in the city. For the most part, he came home late, so I did not spend much time with him either. I learned to be an adult and make decisions independently from an early age, and I believe I felt abandoned, neglected, and unwanted. I did not learn the importance of emotional bonding. Thus, as I grew up, I struggled to fit in yet was emotionally distant. Ultimately, I made wrong decisions in my choice of friends and relationships. Having a sense of belonging was crucial, so much so that I hung out with them even when I was not enjoying myself.

The abandonment I faced in my early childhood shaped my subconscious mind and how I reacted in some situations. The thought of confronting someone made me very anxious, even when I was in the right. I learned not to show much emotion. I never cried; my son has seldom seen me cry. I thought that was a sign of strength, but really it was just an attempt to tune out and suppress or lock away my emotions. Growing up, I didn't have anyone to cry to, so I learned not to. Besides, I was unaware of the health benefits of crying; how emotional tears flush toxins and stress hormones from the body while producing endorphins and oxytocin, the feel-good chemicals that ease emotional and physical pain.

That I survived, that we all survive is a miracle from God. To this day, I believe He was watching over me, knocking on my heart with a desire to provide what I was seeking.

Since trauma changes the way a person's brain works, it is not easy for such a person to say no to the temptation that may lead to addiction as confidently as it is for a regular person. The brain of a traumatized person is simply not equipped to have higher conscious control unless actively pursued.

At around the age of fourteen, I developed an addiction. I discovered that I found comfort in novels, especially romance novels. I could not get enough of the love and happy endings that were portrayed in those books. I would read them day and night, in class, on the bus, and miss sleep just to read. I would read in class and could not wait to finish a lesson or an exam to get my hands on them. I dreamt of meeting a dream man, and the novels were my reality. I overcame my addiction to stories after I graduated high school, but only to replace it with risky behavior, wild friends, and clubbing. I would not call this addiction but notice how my experiences of abandonment shaped my decision-making process. These were my demons, and they haunted me a long time before I realized their presence.

After finding a new way to fill the void of loneliness with friendships, I started spending more time with them. And these were not the regular kind of friends I had back in high school. These were the 'fun' friends. We would often visit clubs and party all night. Despite not liking that lifestyle, I tried to blend in. You see, fitting in fed my need to be accepted and loved.

Unfortunately, the feeling was always short-lived; trying to fill the emotional void this way is never enough. Yet, loneliness always drove me back to seeking these friends and places to dance and have a "fabulous" time. The funny thing is that often I could hardly wait to get away after one night of this. I was experiencing a classic way of solving a problem with a problem and never finding the solution. I believe it is by God's grace that I was never addicted to any substances; I never went to clubs alone. The companionship combined with the dancing was what I always craved; I craved emotional attachments, and movement provided relief. Dancing and movement are known to be therapy for trauma, and they are said to reduce stress and symptoms of anxiety or depression.

Unknowingly, I was seeking belonging and healing. Now that I think about it, things would have been much easier for me if I had known then what I know now. Back then, I was clueless about how our childhood traumas affect us. I had always thought that my actions were entirely of my own. I had no direction and no guidance. I knew about God but did not know Him. My mother was religious, but I never gave much importance to her faith. Instead of healing my pain, I was running from it and believed that this life was the better alternative. If I had any idea how past experiences had affected me and my relationships, I wouldn't have blamed myself so much. Instead, I would have focused on seeking for healing in Christ.

It was not until about a couple of years ago that my life changed when I gave my life to Christ and started studying the Bible. I realized that the previous lifestyle was not mine, and those friends were not real friends. Most, like me, had traumatic experiences. Take Crissy, for example; I could never forget the many times Crissy bitterly complained about her narcissistic mother, who was never content with anything Crissy did; she criticized her for almost everything. And the more she did, the worse Crissy became. Crissy, in turn, tried to please her mother in every way possible, but it was never enough. She was beautiful and intelligent, and she loved her mom, but she did not have great self-esteem. She desired to be liked by everyone but never kept many friends. Crissy also loved to drink and party, and she would some-times become uncontrollable when she did. Sometimes we argued about her insensitivity and self-sabotaging behavior. I did not understand why she behaved this way and could not just ignore her mom, who I thought was mean and self-ish. But we all need our moms, don't we? Just as our sons need us. Crissy was diagnosed with cancer a couple of years ago, and I sometimes wonder at the disease's connection with her childhood.

Anyway, I eventually realized I did not like that lifestyle anymore, and I left it behind and became a Christian about a year later. I knew Christ had been knocking on my heart all along. In Revelation 3:20, He tells us,

> *"Behold I stand at the door, and knock: If any man*
> *hears my voice and opens the door, I will come in*
> *to him and will sup with him, and he with me."*

> — REVELATION 3:20

Christ never forces His way, He knocks, and when we let him in, we must close the door to the temptations of Satan. So, Christ became my friend, confidant and I knew I had found One I could trust. I lost interest in worldly music, dress, 'friends,' unhealthy food, romance novels, and my life was no longer an empty cycle of loneliness and sadness but one of hope, joy, and trust. I even found a new book to read, The Bible, which has the most transformative power than any other book in the world. Saying that the journey has been easy, or without troubles and trials, or that the past doesn't haunt me sometimes would be a lie. However, I am more rational about it and acknowledge that some wounds will always remain, albeit more manageable and less painful. If it were not for God giving me *"peace that passes understand-*

*ing,"* I would have been a total wreck, especially with the experience of my son's substance abuse.

I realize that I was not always available emotionally for my son Alan due to my own deprivation. Because I did not receive emotional nurturing myself, I had no footsteps to follow. My son was also very sensitive, and I tried to toughen him up by cuddling him less and teaching him to be more independent. Although I provided the material needs as much as possible, single parenthood, financial struggles, and lack of wisdom did not help matters. Then due to unavoidable circumstances, when he was only 15 years old, I left him with my family and relocated. Though I left hoping that I would be apart from him only for a short time, the reality was much different, and the years just passed. When I discovered his Marijuana use (and I don't know what else), dropping out of university, lack of motivation, and risky behavior, I painfully realized the full impact of generational trauma and rifts in the family unit.

Now that I recalled those experiences, I realized my son must have gone through a similar type of trauma as I did. Much of my actions were controlled by the subconscious mind as a response to my adversities. The realization came when I spent time reflecting as I tried to understand my son's destructive behavior. The consequences of my traumas hurt my son, who was possibly emotionally deprived and felt abandoned, disengaged from his own emotions, therefore finding comfort in friends who were similarly using substances.

Thus, the cycle is repeated. Unknowingly, we hurt our loved ones by the actions mediated by our traumatic past. Before this incident, I always believed Alan was happy; he was never disrespectful, we rarely quarreled, he seemed to have mature friends, was bright, and did well in school. I believed our relationship was great. Before the addiction, we would talk for hours, yet I never heard the yearning of a son needing his momma; he never complained. He was courageous until he could not be brave anymore.

Have you spent time in reflection? Think about your past. How was it like growing up? Can you recall some traumatic experiences that could have been affecting your behavior? Even if you cannot connect the dots, it could be there, subtly hidden behind "normal."

# 14

# ADVERSE CHILDHOOD
# EXPERIENCES (ACE) QUIZ

A recommended way to know is to take the Adverse Childhood Score test. It is a test consisting of 10 multiple choice questions that help you determine whether you had an adverse childhood or not. While it may feel unnecessary, it is helpful. Because, by identifying your trauma, you can start the healing process and get to a place where you can help your son.

Recognizing childhood adversity is an essential step that helps both you and your son. When you reflect on your own need for acceptance, you will understand your son more and connect to him on a deeper level.

According to Dr. Nadine Burke, Founder of the Center for Youth Wellness, and current Surgeon General of California,

*"Childhood trauma increases the risk for seven out of ten of the leading causes of death in the United States. In high doses, it affects brain development, the immune system, hormonal systems, and even the way our DNA is read and transcribed."*

— DR. NADINE BURKE

She strongly advises taking the Adverse Childhood Experiences (ACE) study test. This study was the first-ever of its kind, conducted on over 17,000 Health Maintenance Organization members. The ACEs test result is not only an indicator of adverse childhood but is also a prediction of the negative effects suffered by the individual in later life. Thus, for any person who has suffered from childhood trauma or has lived in an adverse environment, it is imperative to take the test to assess the damaging effect of trauma on their life.

The ACE test includes experiences of both first-hand and second-hand trauma. Sometimes, people ignore second-hand traumatic experiences because those didn't happen directly to them; instead, they happened to a loved one. For example, my friend Linda who was never hit, was sometimes present when her father struck her mother. When she took the test, her score was 6. The ACES test results helped her to recognize the debilitating effects of witnessing violence. From the results, you know the risks you are facing. A score of 1-3 is lower risk. A score higher than four means that the likelihood of chronic pulmonary lung disease increases 390 percent, hepatitis 240 percent, depression 460 percent, and suicide 1,220 percent. As a mom, you are in the best position to know about your son's childhood experiences and environment, and you may be able to recommend or take it on his behalf.

In the research done on the ACEs test, the factor that may nullify the negative impacts of the ACE on the adoption of health-harming behaviors and lower mental well-being in adulthood was to have access to a trusted adult as a child. The result of the research shows that among the 7,047 participants of the study, those who had AAA [always available adult] support had a lesser prevalence of poor diet or substance abuse. The prevalence was only 7.1% with available adult support, while without, it was 21.5%. People who had none were 30% more likely to engage in self-harming behaviors. This study makes me believe that if my son had a stable, loving adult figure to turn to, he would have been less likely to fall into substance abuse.

So, while I reflected on my life, I contemplated my son's. I thought about all my behaviors and what shaped them. And I thought about all the possible factors that could have traumatized him. I blamed myself for some, kicked myself for some, and acknowledged that some were inevitable, like the many times I did not have a nanny and would leave him with friends while I struggled to look for a job or keep one. Or when I had one and was not sure what happened while I was away. I remember a few times; I asked my boss for an hour or so to go home and check on the baby. I recall at least three times when I found him alone. The door locked, and the nanny gone to have her fun or to visit friends. Obviously, I do not know what happened when I did not have a chance or possibility of going home early. I always felt uneasy leaving, but I had to work.

With practical knowledge comes freedom. When you realize that your struggle is not unique to you; and a relatively common phenomenon and that you cannot blame yourself or get stuck in regret for how you raised your child, you start to gain a sense of control. For example, when I became aware of my abandonment trauma, I saw the possible effects and decided that I would no longer let it control my life. I decided to be more vulnerable and express my faults and seek help. I was more empathetic to my son's substance abuse than if I had not taken the time to go down memory lane. Thankfully, I took the time to forgive and be gentle with myself while studying what the experts had to say.

I gained more insight and control over my reactions, attitude, and responses which helped me take the time to consider how to address the situation. It took a lot of restraining, but the next time I had a conversation with him, I was more empathetic, understanding and although I acknowledged the possible cause, I still let him know that he needed help. I often avoided confrontational or judgmental words, but it was not always easy. Initially, in my panic and fear, I gave him numerous lectures, which were not helping much. My son threatened to block me, which he did many times. I knew that besides the trauma, his situation was causing extreme toxic stress, lack of peace, warmth, and control. He had dropped out of university, lost his apartment, clothing, and except for shattered dreams, he had nothing much going for him. Despite this, he rejected my help many times except to attempt to manipulate me to send him money which I often refused.

It has been challenging, but another promise which says,

> *"I can do all things through Christ which strengtheneth me."*
>
> — PHILIPPIANS 4:13

gives us hope in Christ to beat these demons. I do not believe this is unique to me, but I know mothers who can hardly believe the cruel words their addicted sons throw at them. The venom and anger are beyond words, and it is sometimes difficult to hold your peace. But you must. We know the root of all pain and unhappiness is evil from the devil. Sin is the root cause of all the afflictions we encounter in this life, but sin comes with some occurrence in human lives because it's not a separate entity on its own. So, until there is a desire to be separated from sin and evil, most of our efforts will fail, our sons will get worse, and the cycle will continue.

# STEP #3

## NOURISH YOUR SPIRIT WITH SELF-CARE

# 15

# CHANGE ALWAYS STARTS
# WITH YOU

S o as not to come out as presumptuous, I took the time to understand more about how mothers felt and talked to several of them. The mothers' perspective is not always emphasized or discussed when it comes to addiction. We always care about what the son is feeling, and we devise techniques for dealing with his addiction. But the mother is the one who must remain strong throughout the journey. She gets to cope with everything, the anger, the sorrow, the guilt. That is not to say that other caregivers don't, but this book is a voice speaking to the moms.

And of course, the last chapters were all about understanding and empathizing with your son. Now we must prepare you for the task, and this is where the real work begins.

Change begins with you taking time for yourself and focusing on you. This may surprise you, but the entire family's happiness depends mainly on the mother and wife. In recent years, most relationship coaches have taught wives empowerment skills to change their relationships into what they desire. They are taught how to change themselves, take responsibility for their actions, and how change affects them and their families.

Have you ever noticed the mothers of your support group or those of addicted kids in general? It could also be you; Almost always, you have dark circles under your eyes, constantly tired, mentally more than physically. You start each day early, go to work, come back home, make dinner, worry, check on your son the whole time, wonder where he is and what he is doing. You are exhausted and short-tempered. There is no relief, no end to this struggle. Each day seems to bring new challenges, new mountains to climb, new problems to solve, and your inner battles are apparent on your face and attitude.

No matter the effort you put in, having an addicted teen or young adult son is always a step forward and several steps back. For anyone, this is enough to drive them crazy. Add the daily stress of having to make ends meet and to run a home, and you've got the life of an exhausted, dispirited mother. Being a mom is difficult as it is; the added stress and worry sometimes become too much to handle. You feel as if you have reached your breaking point, almost wishing to go somewhere and hide. Nothing, not even church, gives you the peace it once did. With their 'perfect homes and perfect families, your Christian friends seem to look at you with censure. If this goes on, you may completely burn out or get seriously sick before your son is sober. For his sake, you need to take care of yourself. If you are not strong, you cannot hold your family together. This constant running around trying to change and take care of everybody else drains you faster than you can help them.

Like Mrs. Harper, a fellow member of my support group, Mrs. Harper works 12-16 hours per day to support her family. She has two kids, and as a single parent, her responsibilities are pretty extensive. Even so, she has an enviable work ethic, holds an upper-level position in her company, manages to take care of her sons, and has even bought her first home.

When she learned about her son's addiction problem, she was in denial for a long time. With acceptance, she realized that it was more severe than she thought. Every time she looked at her son, she would lose it. However, she made it her life's goal to help him and protect her other son from the same fate. She had been to seminars, had consulted doctors and psychologists. She had gone to Al-anon meetings, but she still could not seem to have found a solution. While trying to help change her son, she had run herself ragged, lost weight, was unkempt, and did not have time for friends anymore. She snapped at everyone, and her children were afraid to approach or talk to her. One day, she broke down in the group meeting with the news that she might be losing her job. She can't lose that job; her entire family depends on it!

This mom is a classic case of one who has forgotten to take care of herself; her life revolved around her son, yet he seemed to be getting worse despite her attempts to help him. When you are the calm, composed, and happy available adult, your son, will gravitate towards you when they seek a safe place. However, that will only happen when you choose to change and spend time in your self-care. Without it, your relationships get strained because family depends significantly on the mom's energy, whether positive or negative.

In relationships, moms rule, and the secret is to rule wisely. If you obsess with what they say or do, correcting, criticizing, and condemning, trying to fix them, you just end up exhausted, frustrated, and repetitive. The intelligent thing to do is decide to let go of the need to control outcomes and spend more time working on your happiness, attitude, and perception. Too often, we focus on what others should do, speak or act differently, and never take the time to consider what role we play in influencing them.

Unfortunately, mothers and women in general, due to our nurturing nature, put our needs last while everyone else goes first. We think that if we were to stop, were not on top of the game, taking charge and making sure everything runs smoothly, the whole family would crumble. This life goes on for years, and there is never a good time to relax and take care of yourself. You possibly don't see how you can take time for yourself when a much more urgent issue is pressing: in this case, your son who is spiraling out of control. However, only a healed person can heal another. Do you remember how we talked about childhood trauma? People who have suffered through it at an early age suffer through developmental deficiencies. They often do not recognize an adverse environment themselves as it is so common and normal to them. Their children, in turn, suffer because their parents are unable to recognize any instability in their family.

Honestly, if one was raised in a disengaged environment, it is impossible to spot the missing little things: the absence of hugs and kisses, spending time as a family, praying and reading the bible, enjoying TV shows, eating ice cream, goofing around, being vulnerable, independent thinking, etc. A mom may not know that she is missing anything by not practicing these things or is so busy or stressed that there just hasn't been any time. And she may think nothing of it. But a few weeks become years, and suddenly there is an emotional gap between the children and the mom. Now, not to point fingers or to say that there is anyone to blame here. Nevertheless, we must recognize that when a parent is too stressed or has unresolved emotional or mental issues, their children face the consequences.

How else can this generational cycle of pain and dysfunction end in families unless someone informed stops it? During reflection, you may have realized that some experiences from your past could have caused emotional distress to your child or that your child could have had a traumatic experience you had no control over. And now he is an addict, and you are exhausted trying to help him. How about you take a step back, heal your emotional scars, and lay them to rest as you heal your current emotional turmoil through self-care?

For most mothers, nay for all mothers, this first step is the most difficult. And it requires much patience. How can you possibly change what you have been doing for years and take time for yourself? What if something happens? Does it feel like you are failing your son or even cheating him of attention for thinking this way? Remember, your emotional and physical health reflects on your children. When you are well adjusted and emotionally secure, they will feel confident and safe as well. For a troubled son, safety is tremendously valuable and is the first thing you can offer. You may need to first get off his back and focus on you. When your addicted son feels acceptance, love, understanding, and no judgment from his family, the home will be the place he feels safe. The goal is not to feel the need to leave the home environment or seek drugs when he feels scared or overwhelmed anymore; instead, he comes to you. And this applies to any human being. We are created social, always in need of acceptance in happy and healthy relationships.

Whether you had a difficult childhood, marriage, or think you could have done better raising your kids, the most important thing is that you have been seeking to solve the problem at hand. As you may have noticed, *The 7 Steps to Help Your Son in Addiction Recovery* are not a quick-fix program. Neither you nor your son will change overnight, trust will not grow immediately, and he will not stop saying cruel things or yelling obscenities instantly. There will still be tears, frustrations, and a desire just to let him do whatever he wants, but as long as you don't give up and do the right thing, you will harvest results.

Besides, there is only so much a mom can do. Some things are and will always be out of your control; your addicted son may still reject all the love and support you provide. As mothers, we tell ourselves, "With a little more effort, I can help my son" or "If I do this, I can correct my son." See, you can do all the right things, provide a good home and guidance, but do not forget that ultimately your son is the one who decides to come back to the right path. And you are his shepherd, but you cannot take his steps for him. And taking a break now and then and doing things you love will not prevent his progress.

## FORGIVE AND FORGET

Moving from the past is critical, whether from pain experienced in childhood or recent unpleasant experiences. You are starting afresh, where no shadow of the past taints your soul—the deleterious effects of the previous trauma left behind as you move forward. Nevertheless, moving forward is a feat suggested by many but achieved by few.

Leaving the memories behind and, along with them, all bitterness, anger, and anxiety takes time. But consciously working on healing fades them away, and the pain abates. When Jesus lived here on earth, He spent most of His time healing the sick, some who had suffered for years, like the woman with the issue of blood. She has seen all kinds of physicians, and none had been able to help her until, with faith, she touched the garment of The Master Physician. Do you suppose she had mental anguish as well or forgot the 12 painful years? No! but she was able to tell the story without experiencing the emotional pain of those years. It is not because people don't have bad experiences; it's how they allow those experiences to shape or affect them in their current lives.

How do you move forward while those who hurt you have not acknowledged their guilt or apologized? The Bible says,

> *"Not rendering evil for evil, or railing for railing:*
> *but contrariwise blessing; knowing that ye are*
> *thereunto called, that ye should inherit a*
> *blessing."*

> — 1 PETER 3:9

The people who have hurt you may never realize that they did, or if they do, they may be too embarrassed to acknowledge it and ask for forgiveness. For your own sake, it is better to forget the offense and forgive.

When you forgive, you are not only letting your aggressor free but setting yourself free as well. You are cutting the pain that connects you two, closing that chapter of your life, and allowing yourself to be born anew.

Forgiveness is a step most people struggle with before they can move on. When we blame someone close to us, when we hold the hurt and the anger inside, we somehow blame ourselves too. Feeling that we could have done things differently, and while this may be true, we cannot change the past, that's why forgiveness should start with you forgiving yourself. When you come to this stage and realize the damage you have unknowingly done to yourself and your relationships, forgive and find the grace to be kind to yourself. Most moms treat themselves in a way they would never treat another human being; they are too hard and unforgiving to themselves. If you cannot love or forgive yourself first, you may not be able to forgive your offender and start your healing process. You may have lost control then, but today you have control of your words and actions; let go, give yourself a reprieve from the outrage, guilt, and blame and move on.

So, are you ready to forgive your addicted son? Yes, even for the unmentionable words he uttered or for hitting you or stealing from you. There is nothing you cannot pardon, even if your son had done the same hurtful things repeatedly. In Matthew 18:21-22, Peter wanted to know how many times he should forgive his brother, he thought seven times were plenty, but Jesus corrected him. Verse 22 says Jesus saith unto him, *"I say not unto thee, until seven times: but, until seventy times seven,"* simply put, you cannot hold a grudge and be happy; justified or not.

By now, I believe you understand your son's struggle better, and although you cannot clear him of all the guilt of his words and actions, let him know that some things he said or did have been painful, but that you forgive and still love him. Details are not necessary at this point. Just because he is an addict does not mean he doesn't have a conscience or cannot understand; it is the approach that matters.

You can ask him to forgive you, and although he might do something terrible again, your job is to maintain your composure and spirit of forgiveness.

Did I say this is hard work?

I did!

Moms who have learned self-care get better results, and although it may be challenging, it gets easier with practice. Each step may take one year or close, but there is hope if your son is not running in the other direction. Your goal is to have him recover, maybe get to rehab, or heal from trauma, and in the process, heal yourself too.

Let us be practical then, so far you have understood your son, identified your errors, forgiven, what next?

## HAPPINESS! AN INSIDE JOB

Self-care comes with the realization that only when happy can you make others happy. When you stop doing what others expect of you and do what you know to be true; it makes you feel beautiful, adorable, energized, blessed, and radiant, then you are on the path to happiness and health. Others will draw your positive energy, just as they have been drawing on your negative energy. As I mentioned earlier, moms influence how relationships turn out in the family especially mother-son relationships. It is funny, but the whole family is affected. When mom is sad, stressed, and angry, suddenly children are selfish, rude, and defensive, yet they can't keep away from her. Why this happens is mysterious to me.

When your son sees how unhappy, stressed, or sick you are, he gets worse. You would think that he would be hit by remorse, feel sorry for you, and strive to change. But the very opposite happens; he drowns more into his addiction, and you are left feeling more hurt and resentful. As we have established, he is going through a difficult time, full of shame and guilt for the stress he cannot handle or the emotional turmoil he cannot deal with; how do you suppose he can handle yours? The secret here is to strive to be happy. Your happiness takes one load off his back. It may be hard to believe, but he wants to keep you that way, and with time, he may strive to get better, seek help, or attempt to quit. When he starts to respond better to you, you are on the way to recovery.

The happier you are, the easier this journey will be.

I saw this transformative process with Ann; the last time I went to see her, I noticed she was laughing more, was relaxed, chatty, and seemed upbeat and vibrant. She told me that she was spending more time with her husband, and they had been visiting places together. Her son, Luke, who for a few years had yelled hurtful words, growled at her, and basically ignored most of what she ever asked him to do, was now spending more time with the family. Before, he would stay locked up in his room for days, only getting out for something to eat. He hardly spoke with anyone, and when he did, he was extremely vulgar. He had dropped out of high school, refused to go to college or get a job. See, he was addicted to the internet.

Of course, Ann and her family had prayed a lot too, but it wasn't until she got off Luke's back and took a hard look at how she had been reacting to him that she was able to start helping him. She slowly spent time in self-care, and she was happy and started communicating naturally with him without any judgment or criticism. The young man began to warm up and slowly become chatty and respectful. He had not quit his addiction, there were milestones to cross, but at least Ann and her son could have a decent conversation. I hadn't asked Ann yet, but I knew that her change of attitude had a lot to do with it. Her husband seemed happier too; he was laughing a lot. All in all, Ann was getting back the family she desired.

So how do you get on this journey?

Remember a time you were happy, the sensations you felt, the sparkle in your eye, the brightness of your smile. When was the last time you allowed such joy in your life? What was happening at that time? To regain memory, put pen to paper, write down things you did, and consider reviving them. Honestly, they don't have to be things that will tone your muscles or make the house look like a magazine picture, but those that make you happy doing them at that moment. They could be things like taking a nap, reading a devotional or book, chatting with a friend, or celebrating a milestone. The list is endless.

Maybe you haven't done any of these things in a long time and wonder what to write. Keeping a journal and writing down anything that comes to mind is very helpful. Then practice **doing three of those** things every day.

You don't have time? Surely you can make time for your happiness and sanity!

I love listening to music, soaking in a bath, walking in nature, or basking in the sun. These activities are nothing earth-shattering, but they are essential. I have learned not to get riddled with guilt or consider this as poor use of quality time, as I know you probably do, but I have realized that after some good Christian hymns, I am in a better mood, not easily rattled. So, take time for yourself; lose yourself in whatever makes you happy. It could be the haircut you have been putting off, a meeting with your girl-friend for a chat, or a round in the gym, do it and come back rejuvenated and happy. Remember to do the three things every day!

There will be bumps and days when you are tempted to give up, but if your son says something rude, keep on track, he does something annoying, keep in your lane. It is less exhausting to be positive and happy. If you still don't know what to do for your happiness, find a hobby; it could be an interest you have been putting off for years, like learning an instrument or crocheting.

## NOT EASILY TRIGGERED

As you get happier and more relaxed, do you realize you are healing your emotions? Often, we get strung up with emotions, marinating about something someone said or did, getting more and more agitated or angry, and when your son comes home drunk again, you just explode. You get triggered easily, and while you could have avoided him because you know how he gets when drunk, you end up antagonizing him, exchanging words, and getting hurt in the process. I often felt the urge to retort with something sarcastic or hurtful when my son said something nasty, but I have had to bite my tongue many times and say something less triggering instead.

You see, you control your emotions depending on how happy you are because you change your perception of the other individual. If you think your son is doing something to hurt you, it will hurt, and even if he is doing it with intent to hurt you, it is up to you to rise or not rise to the bait. You will notice his animosity diminishes, and the temper cools down when you don't tango with him. It takes courage not to do what you feel naturally inclined to do, but you are a courageous mom, aren't you?

## REPLENISH YOUR HEALTH

Someone once told me, 'Moms don't get sick,' And I believed that. When you get sick, who will take care of everybody else? You ask.

Well, health is the most important asset you have besides God and family, and often as a mom, it is easy to ignore some aches and pains if they do not prevent you from daily activities. Unfortunately, the body absorbs the stress and beatings until one day it just gives in, and you get sick.

So, is it a cold? Curl up in bed and let someone else take care of you and the home; call off work. Maybe you worry that others won't cook or clean or worry about your son's where-abouts like you would. But any ailment is a sign that the body needs a break and help to rejuvenate. Many moms have got critically sick for not giving their bodies time to heal yet expect to have the strength to help in their son's recovery. You can only keep going for so long.

I was invited to a health retreat in September 2021 during the Labor Day weekend. I immediately signed up, and then as the days were drawing closer, I started to have regrets. I thought taking five days off work and working on this book was a colossal waste of time. I carried my laptop in the hope of having moments of relief to sit and use it. However, I am so grateful we had plenty of activities. I enjoyed the clean, crisp mountain air of Pike National Forest of Colorado, fresh organic food, new friends, early bedtime, and morning worship with my group. The shocking thing was that I had persistent lower back pain, and by the time I got back home, it was gone! 98% of the pain was gone; my night flashes and sweats were gone. It was amazing. I had often heard of the importance of spending time in nature and did it often, maybe for a day or two, but I had not experienced this kind of healing before. The health benefits of this retreat were almost instantaneous and obvious. So maybe all you need is to take a break and disappear for a couple of days if you feel sick and tired; oh, and did I tell you, we had no phone service!

Health is mainly about the quality of your life. Is your food fresh and nutritious, are your relationships healthy, do you have a spiritual life, enjoy your career, movement? It is not just about food; it is about having all your physical, emotional, spiritual, and mental needs well balanced and working together.

## TIME IN SOLITARY

Men are said to go into 'their cave,' and nobody should venture in, even their wives. It is a time of reflection, gathering thoughts, or thinking of nothing at all. Why should moms not have the same? Leave the mess behind and go to a place unknown? When I left for Colorado, I had a thousand things to do and deadlines to meet, but I unknowingly needed the break.

Granted, I do not have younger children to take care of, but I know moms to be resourceful, and you can find someone to keep an eye on them. It is especially a good time to connect with God if you are spiritually inclined, get in a car or plane, turn off the phone and sit by a river or beach somewhere and just talk to Him. With all the cares of life and people demanding your attention, it's almost impossible to consider this as time well spent. It may not seem like it is worth it, but in addition to all the other self-care, taking time to declutter your mind, let it slow down, and reconnect with yourself, can train you to let go of the need to be strong, in control and in charge of everything.

In addition to the occasional getaway, take a day off every seven days.

> *"And God blessed the seventh day, and sanctified it: because that in it he had rested from all his work which God created and made."*

> — GENESIS 2:3

It is not because God was tired, but for our sake, He blessed and sanctified the day of rest because He knew how much we needed it. Not only is rest a biblical principle, but it is also a requirement. It allows time to commune with God, improve relationships, ensure a day free of distractions for family time, and improve physical health as we heal from stress or injury.

According to Dr. Matthew Sleeth, an author, and doctor, he used to get so exhausted after a 24-hour Sunday shift until he decided to take Saturday off and adopt the 24/6 principle that changed his life. He became more relaxed and productive.

People had a day of rest throughout history, but this changed, and people started to work nonstop. Instead of doing better, more people became depressed, anxious, and stressed because of working without rest. Constant stress has adverse psychological effects that cause reactions to the hormonal system as it produces much adrenalin, which keeps the body constantly stressed prepared for fight or flight.

So, when is your next getaway? It could be a day or a week. Plan a trip and pack a bag.

## AVOID TOXIC PEOPLE

'Misery loves company.' When sad, you may be drawn to sad people. Then you spend hours talking about all your problems, magnifying them, and spoiling your mood. People often have opinions that may be harmful advice that causes greater rifts with your son. It is time to cut those conversations about your family life. Anyone who makes you feel drained and ill-tempered or like a bad mother should be avoided. They may be family, and you must love them, but your problems should not materialize unless someone is looking to help fix something or pray. With all that is happening, toxic, sullen, morose, unhappy people are the last thing you need.

Besides, when you are constantly happy, toxic people have zero advantage over you, and eventually, they leave you alone, and if they don't, maybe it's time to think about changing friends, jobs, or moving.

## WHY WORRY?

How does one constantly keep happy and worry-free with all the stress and frustration? When giving the sermon on the mount, Jesus asked,

> *"Which of you by worrying can add one cubit to his stature?"*

— MATTHEW 6:27 (NKJV)

Here Jesus was talking about the vanity of anxiety and worry, especially about the future. Worry has never solved any problem or prevented an incident from happening. But it has caused sickness and loss of peace. To alleviate worry, consider using that energy and time in a happy activity unless you have a problem you can actually solve.

I remember the many nights I lost sleep, waking up in panic, heart pounding, worried, and scared for my son. Afraid to read texts from my cousin, who he was living with at the time. Then I remembered learning in my bible study that worrying is a sin, a lack of faith. You cannot pray and worry. I learned to pray fervently, really pray, claim Bible promises and plead for peace.

Soon I was able to have a whole night's sleep. It was not because my son had improved and stopped running wild or using. It was because I got *"peace beyond understanding."* At first, I felt guilty and alarmed, trying to resume the burden of distress and worry. I almost felt like I had no right to feel this way. I knew I cared deeply for my son because whenever I prayed or spoke about him, I cried, but it is incredible what God can do when you faithfully put your worries and concerns on His capable shoulders. So, you don't know where your son is, what he is doing, or who with? Pray and go to sleep.

## ADOPT THE SPIRIT OF GRATITUDE

And finally, develop a spirit of gratitude, sure the world seems to be falling apart, your son's addiction, family problems, sickness, loss of jobs, earthquakes, diseases, and a host of bad things happening. But there are still things to offer gratitude. It may not seem like it but think about it. Aren't you grateful to be reading this book, renewing hope? What else are you grateful for? Think of three things, and every day when you wake up, journal your gratitude, and soon you will have hundreds of them.

If still struggling to adopt this lifestyle, do it often. Practice makes things perfect, and don't forget to look for support groups around you if you are not in one already. Accept your limits, admit that you need support. Do not pretend to be strong when you are broken inside. Acknowledging your weaknesses does not mean you have accepted defeat; it just means you are human. Join a church, a fellowship group, a prayer group, or any kind of social group and talk to other mothers. After all, you know more than they do from reading and applying *The 7 Steps to Help Your Son in Addiction Recovery.*

# STEP #4

## COMMUNICATION

# IMPORTANCE OF COMMUNICATION

S creaming matches had become common in the Jones' household. Now, the Jones live in a reputable residential area. While the occurrence of an occasional fight now and then is considered normal, loud, heated arguments every day are frowned upon. Mrs. Jones knows it and is extremely uncomfortable and irritated with the whole situation.

The fights are usually between herself and her son, who she has known to use opioids. She is embarrassed and baffled about what to do. Mrs. Jones is even angrier that every time she wants to talk to her son Ethan about it, he straight out gets rude and defensive. He yells profanities, is constantly irritated with her, and she can never get a decent conversation out of him. "I hate you, and I hate living in this house," are some of the things neighbors can hear Ethan yelling. For the life of her, the hurt Mrs. Jones cannot figure out why her son is so annoyed and rude. She finds herself yelling back and has nothing to show for it except tension and deep resentment towards her son. Why can't he just talk to her? She is trying to help him, isn't she?

In most homes with an addict, communication is often so broken that the pain it causes is almost palpable. No one stops to listen to the other person. Arguments and fights are common, anger and insults are the order of the day, yet unless this approach changes, there will be rifts that cannot be mended.

Addiction is so stigmatized in our culture that addicts anticipate others to condemn, ridicule, degrade and reject them. Because of the broken trust, they do not turn to the one person they should communicate with. They feel unheard and misunderstood; they isolate from loved ones, especially the mom, yet as heartbreaking as it is, she still must find a way to reach him through proper communication.

If you have spent any time in self-care, you will realize the futility of getting emotional every time your son does something selfish or unacceptable. A lot must change in the home environment.

And what better way than changing your communication style?

*"He that is slow to wrath is of great understanding:*
*but he that is hasty of spirit exalteth folly."*

— PROVERBS 14:29

The change would include much self-control.

While communication in relationships is said to be impera-tive, it is often overrated. Most moms believe that communi-cation is talking endlessly to their sons about the addiction and his bad behavior; that it involves lecturing, criticizing, judging, condemning, insulting, and all the while expecting him to change. There are many ways to communicate, whether it's through body language, silence, and of course, words that can be detrimental or beneficial to relationships. When your son is under the influence, words may be the last way he would want to communicate, especially if he feels misunderstood, condemned, or attacked. This frustration often causes irritability and defensiveness. When he feels scared and miserable, he may want to go to an adult or a safe place, so it is vital that your conversation is loving, brief, and as specific as possible.

Ethan likes to go to his room for shelter, as he feels some-what safe there. He no longer associates his mom, home, or family as a safe and comfortable place, and he cannot communicate that he needs help. It would be great if you made communication easy for your addicted son and made him feel encouraged and validated. He needs to realize he is not beyond help and that he is not a bad person. Whatever problem he is facing, he needs to be able to make you understand it. Remember, it is crucial for him to feel safe, understood, and not judged.

The goal of taking these seven steps is to help you help your son in his recovery. And if he still needs it, get the professional help he needs. Sometimes he may quit without any professional therapy when you follow these steps. Either way, keep going, whatever the frustration. It is all right to express how you feel as long as you keep it peaceful and factual. For example, saying, 'I was worried when you didn't come home last night." Who knows? Your son may actually be empathetic towards you. While remorse and empathy seem prominently absent with a user, your kindness should remain consistent.

As incredible as the outcomes of being able to communicate with your son may seem, this is going to be an assiduous process for you. Like everything else, it requires much self-restraint, and I cannot promise you that he will always cooperate. In many cases, a decent conversation may not be expected between a substance abuser and his mom. It may not happen all the time; in fact, it will not happen often, but it is progress nonetheless.

Choosing a time to communicate when he is not under the influence is critical. Determine who should be present or not present when talking with your son. Some members of the family may antagonize the situation while others motivate and encourage him.

There are days when he doesn't want to talk with you or anyone, and that's okay; it's part of the process. Keep your peace and live to address any issue some other time. Other times he may still say hurtful things to test or guilt-trip you. Your response or reaction will determine how the conversation will go for the most part.

Often, as I have heard from some moms that "he lies a lot;" it's not a strange thing. When you deny him, he accuses you of using it as leverage to control him. That may be so, but if he cannot account for what he had done before with the money you gave him, then it's time to put on the brakes and let him know your decision. It is unnecessary to deny your son if he needs support, but with substance abuse, trust is broken, and you cannot rebuild it by indulging him. Remember, a substance user can be very resourceful when he wants something. The safer route would be to ask questions and offer alternatives. Like if he wants money for his phone bill, you can offer to pay. Will he like that? Probably not, but he quickly will realize that you are always prepared. The questioning may lead to the real reason he was asking for the money.

When he senses love and empathy in your tone, he softens. He sees your love as unconditional. If God had loved us conditionally, no one would be saved. God says,

*"Love suffers long and is kind; love does not envy; love does not parade itself, is not puffed up; does not behave rudely, does not seek its own, is not provoked, thinks no evil; does not rejoice in iniquity, but rejoices in the truth; bears all things, believes all things, hopes all things, endures all things."*

— CORINTHIANS 13:4-7 (NKJV)

Only through the power of God can humanity love this way. Among us, love is conditional for the most part. When a child misbehaves, he is ignored or punished. An addict son by no means meets a mother's expectations, and it is easy to enable, ignore, reject, stop encouraging, or supporting him. Unfortunately, this creates more problems, yet lovingly seeking why he behaves the way he does should be the goal. If a mom would look beyond the addiction and as much as possible communicate with as much compassion, empathy, and love as her son desires, it may do more than any therapy could. It offers the peace and power he craves and creates a desire to do better.

Unconditional love is enough to communicate without emphasizing the outcome by just letting the conversation flow. By now, he should know that all you desire is for him to recover and live his best life. It will take time, but the results are massive.

Remember, it is fatal to assume you know your son completely. It could be that he only agrees with you because he found out what you like or what you expect of him. With proper conversation where you are gleaning information from him, you may be surprised that he never liked football at all; he only played because his dad insisted. Let your son soar and find his way with you, only offering suggestions that may help him realize the importance of taking responsibility for his future goals more seriously than if he waited for you to direct his path.

Have faith in the Lord and ask for help,

> *"...prayer and supplication, with thanksgiving let your requests be made unto God."*

— PHILIPPIANS 4:6

Then, with love and care, you will be able to reach your son's inner soul.

## ASK QUESTIONS

When in active addiction, I felt like I did not know my son anymore. Besides the distance, communication with him was difficult. I could not get him to say much, so I learned very little of what he was going through. I mainly depended on relatives, my intuition, and reflecting on what his words meant. And I have heard many mothers say the same thing:

the child they were seeing was not the same child they raised. So how would you reconnect and mend what is broken in your relationship and figure out what you can do to communicate without sparks flying?

One of the most crucial aspects of communication is asking questions, not in a critical or judgmental manner, but in a curious, gentle way. I know this as the most challenging thing for moms because we assume we understand or have the solutions, which often include sending him to rehab as fast as possible. We spend countless hours telling him what he should and should not do. It could also be that he remains elusive to the point where it gets difficult to communicate. You will get more out of him when you learn to ask questions that require more than a yes or no response. People and your son is no exception, crave healthy attention, and they are more willing to respond when they sense no condemnation. The best questions should be open-ended questions that create room for more words. Close-ended questions make communication an uphill struggle, and not much is gleaned through this process.

For example, a question like

Do you think I should still give you money? May elicit a YES or NO answer while asking 'What do you find unfair in my not giving you money anymore?' will get a proper response to build your conversation further.

My Health Coaching teacher *Joshua Rosenthal* called them high mileage questions. They are probing, curious yet gentle questions that help individuals open up and reveal information that otherwise would not have come up. Unfortunately, we often ask our sons questions and are too eager to offer advice before knowing what they need to say. Sometimes your son just needs validation, proof that he has been heard. The questioning would also make him pause and help him really think of what he is saying.

If he had responded to 'What do you find unfair in my not giving you money anymore?' with 'Because I feel like you are trying to control me.' Then you would have an opportunity to ask, "If you were in my shoes, what would you have done?' He may pause and think about the answer.

Now, this is not to say that all conversations with this line of questioning will run smoothly; sometimes, they will go south fast. Remember, you are the person coming between him and his addiction, and you are most likely not his most favorite person. It is imperative that he knows he can trust you not to hurt him emotionally. By this time, I am assuming you take time in your self-care and are not easily triggered, able to intuitively tell when to ask questions and when to back off. This kind of attention where he knows you are seeking to understand how you can help him is what he really needs from you.

Your goal in seeking to communicate is to regain the trust in your child, understand him, reduce his irritation toward you, and notice that despite all the inconvenience he causes, you are right there with him. Eventually, he will see that you want him to be happy and believe that he can open up to you. The key is consistency; your son often craves your validation, and he does not like feeling dominated. Asking questions and seeking to understand is a sure way to help him get out of his shell.

## LISTEN MORE

Listening is considered the most crucial aspect of communication, yet people simply do not listen in today's society. When having a conversation with someone, they are often waiting for an opportunity to say something in response, not hearing what you have to say. They are eagerly wondering when you should finish or stop so that they can say something.

"You never listen to me!" How many times has your son told you this? And what is the typical response? "Oh, I listen! you are the one who never listens." Maybe it's time to listen to him instead of accusing him. Ninety percent of the time, he will not do what you ask him to, yet he will accuse you of not listening. These are usually painful times, but you know that he is doing it out of his pain. He is hurting and so hurts you. As most addicted people are not fully aware of this, they cannot control their impulses. After all, how can you control something when you don't know what is driving you to it?

When your son feels that you hear and understand him, he will respond better.

It is unnecessary to psychoanalyze everything he says; rather, it is about asking simple questions and listening to the responses. Some comments, even those yelled in anger or even through lies, can give excellent insight. You know your son better than everybody else, even if he is seemingly weird, so with time and tolerance, you will see the patterns shift as you seek to get the message he is trying to portray or the emotions he is trying to express.

If he yelled something like, "I hate you, you make my life hell." He is trying to express something. Your calm response can be, "I understand you are angry at me right now; what made you feel that I make your life hell?" A typical response from an angry mom would be, "You are very ungrateful, I have provided everything you need, and I am trying to help you." Or something along those lines...

So here you are, affirming that you heard him and are open to discussing it. You are also admitting that you are human and make mistakes too, and you may be surprised at how his defensiveness diminishes. Affirming followed by questions show that you are present and listening, and it may help your son organize his cluttered thoughts into something coherent as he attempts to communicate.

As you listen and affirm what your son is saying, restate what he has just said by repeating his comment. Here you are reflecting on the comment, and when he hears it coming from your mouth, he confirms or denies that was what he meant.

For example, he may say, "I really hate what alcohol is doing to me."

Your thoughtful response would be, "You feel like alcohol is destroying your life."

When you change your communication style and practice active listening, you get more out of your son than if you asked open-ended questions or accused him in response. So he lies, manipulates, or seems to be delusional? That's expected with most substance abusers. Probing, affirming, repeating back what he says, and active listening will guide you to what exactly he is trying to convey. Sometimes you must give him the benefit of the doubt; it doesn't solve much by calling him on his lies except getting him defensive. He will soon realize you are not taken in by them, nor are you agitated by his fluctuating mood.

# WHAT TO COMMUNICATE

## OFFER INFORMATION

As I gathered information about addiction and its connection with trauma, I would send it to my son. It's like I had discovered gold! I would send him text after text of information. At some point, he told me he was fed up with my psychology studies, and I had to back off. Interestingly, he wasn't reacting to all the information I sent him, so I safely assumed he was reading it.

While I wouldn't recommend anyone to offer information the way I did, I would still insist that you should be well informed and ready if you can share something of importance with your son. When I told my son to seek help, I knew what the process would involve and my role in it. He often rejected the offer of rehab, but some of the information I shared must have struck a chord in him because he started to respond. I was telling him of all the possible reasons he and his friends could have experienced trauma. I shared much, but I soon realized that some of the information shook him. He got angry and even worse for some days to the point where he blocked me, and I didn't hear from him, but he unblocked me after some weeks and chatted with me as if nothing had happened.

So, although he may reject your offer of information, you can still share much between your conversations. Having a video or document handy just in case he says yes to the information you may have could prove helpful. The same applies to opinions, although the best approach is to ask if he would be interested to hear what you have to share. When he is treated like a responsible adult, able to accept or reject, he will strive to be such in real life. Confirming that he understood the information offered is also important as it would help you recognize whether he is listening or just humoring you.

## MAKE CONSTRUCTIVE REQUESTS

Sometimes a mom chooses not to bother her addicted son and ignores him to avoid confrontations. She prefers to do all her chores or run errands, which leaves her exhausted and irritable. In response, the boy gets less motivated and more isolated. If things need to be done, a mom should request without fear of his anger or rejection. It is true, he may not do it, but even the laziest person still feels motivated when asked for an opinion or help with something. For example: Ask him the kind of flowers he would like in a vase or where you should place a new piece of furniture. Ask for help to do these things and give duties for cooking, cleaning, and the like. These small ways of making requests will grow a sense of usefulness in him. Do not be surprised if these requests fall on deaf ears because it is also essential to consider his upbringing. If he was raised feeling valuable and helpful at a young age, he might now respond better to your requests than if he was used to feeling entitled or ignored.

## RECOGNITION AND EMPATHY

Sometimes when we look at our addicted children, we find it hard to see the person they could be and instead see what addiction has done to them. I was holding a video conversation with my son, and I couldn't get my mind off how care-worn he looked. He seemed older than his age, thin and weak. However, you have to look past what he is right now and keep focused on what he could be. That makes it easier to tell him with the assurance that there is hope and he is neither stupid nor hopeless. That is how Jesus saw us, not as the filthy rags marred by sin, but what we could be, covered by His righteousness. He trod the path we walk, and He empathizes with our infirmities. So it is with your son, hard as it may be, to get past his current state and the pain he has caused; he needs you to recognize his pain, be empathetic, compassionate, and give him hope for a better tomorrow, whether through words or actions.

## POSITIVE REINFORCEMENTS

While communicating with your boy, you will often realize that your motivation for change may be higher than his motivation for change. Rehabilitation and other treatments may seem very intimidating and challenging for him. So, although he may appear rebellious, it could signify that he is scared, embarrassed, ashamed, and guilty. Keeping him motivated can be an excellent way to bond, and when ready, he may need you to go with him to the therapy sessions and join in the recovery process.

It is improbable that your son is all bad, that you cannot see anything good to say about him. Even the worst people sometimes do something nice. If he did a small positive or generous thing, reward him with a compliment. It could be something he is supposed to do anyway, but because he has not been doing it, when he does, it would be worth taking note and mentioning it. For example, "I noticed you washed your plate today; that was nice." He will strive to do more. Sometimes you may get him a gift or take the day off and spend it with him. Whatever you choose to acknowledge your pride and joy with his improvement, show it and comment on it. Even one day of coming home sober or spending time with family is worth a mention or a compliment and a prayer of gratitude.

Trust that you will get through this. God sometimes allows difficulties in our lives because He knows we can overcome them when we depend on Him.

God tells us,

> *"There hath no temptation taken you but such as is common to man: but God is faithful, who will not suffer you to be tempted above that ye are able; but will with the temptation also make a way to escape, that ye may be able to bear it."*

> — 1 CORINTHIANS 10:13

Keep up the courage, and do not lose faith. With God's help, you can save your son from any means of destruction. Difficulties are the speed bumps you will encounter along the way to you and your son's recovery. Remember, he may seem to have lost his ways, but your place in his heart remains.

## PREDICTABLE APPROACH

Addicts are unpredictable with their words and actions, and thus they are not used to having a predictable aura around them. The friends they have are as unpredictable as their behaviors. Finding predictable positive vibes at home may be what draws your son to realize how empty the world outside can be. When he knows he can come home and find peace or talk to you without you overreacting, he may be more inclined to respond to you positively.

## NON-VERBAL COMMUNICATION

We have all heard the adage that *'Actions speak louder than words.'* Sometimes you do not have to say anything for someone to realize you are upset or happy. Your body posture can say it all. According to helpguide.org,

---

*"Body language is the use of physical behavior, expressions or mannerisms to communicate nonverbally, often done instinctively rather than consciously."*

— HELPGUIDE.ORG

---

It continues to say that your body language can send powerful messages that can draw people towards us or offend and push them away. Examples of body language are posture (are your arms by your side or folded?), eye contact, gestures, voice tone, expression, or silence.

If you are trying to communicate with your son and your words do not match your body language, he will pick on that and react negatively because your thoughts are not aligned with your feelings. You may be thinking you would like to ask your son some questions but feel so hostile towards him because he probably did or said something offensive earlier. Chances are this will come out nonverbally, so do not be surprised when he reacts negatively. Thoughts and feelings need to be aligned to communicate with a person abusing substances as their survival instinct is very high. Do you see how taking time for your self-care is important? Even your communication style changes.

Overall, healthy communication is a vital step, and the easier a mom can make it, the better and faster the results.

# STEP#5

## BOUNDARIES

# 18

# SETTING BOUNDARIES

Setting boundaries when dealing with an addict is a common term. As discussed in chapter six, addiction is a process, and things can get out of control quickly. You may feel that your son is stepping all over you and are unsure how to get things back in control. It is time to set boundaries, but it will take some work, like everything that involves helping him.

Your son may get angry, violent, and more disrespectful as you attempt to establish boundaries, but you must stand firm. If you are spending quality time in self-care, you will find it easier to deal with his fluctuating moods, accusations, and insults in a peaceful manner. It may not seem possible, but even in deep addiction, your son can still listen to reason depending on how you raised him (did you let him get away with bad behavior, or were you overly strict)? And the approach you use.

With all the changes in addiction, we can safely assume that some tensions and tempers are flaring around. Maybe even a sense of loss of control, guilt, and embarrassment in you as a mom, but that there is confusion and emotional turmoil, is without a doubt.

I spoke to the mom of a recovered addict son recently, and she told me that while she was firm with boundaries, her husband gave him whatever he asked for. She saw he was getting worse but felt unable to change the tide. They were not on the same page with her husband, and her son believed she was the enemy. He was very hostile towards her and would not listen to a word she said. Today he is married and a good Christian man who now motivates the young people in his church.

But what are boundaries in relation to addiction? According to Peaks Recovery, boundaries are "*a fence between two or more individuals with the sole purpose of establishing guidelines for actions, responsibilities and encouraging proper behaviors.*" Despite most moms' fears, boundaries allow for healthy relationships. Poor boundaries often lead most moms to compromise and enable their addicted sons, which takes away their peace, lose control of their feelings, freedom, and personal space and property.

## DETERMINE YOUR BOUNDARIES

When you decide to set up boundaries, you will first determine what is acceptable and what is not and find the appropriate time to have a quiet discussion with your son about it.

Depending on your son's habit, it could be no smoking in the house or no meals after everyone else has had dinner. The addictions are different, and the home environment is unique too. However, it would be practical to involve the rest of the family and discuss how you can help establish boundaries to help him and the rest of the family. Other family members may have been crossing the line, so boundaries should apply to them as well. You should be seen as the authority, a strong support, someone to be depended on at a time of crisis. This way, there is no confusing your kindness with gullibility.

Timing is vital, so, if possible, choose a time when the family is present, and your son is not under the influence, or he is in a good mood. Even in substance abuse, there are good and bad days. By this time, the whole family hopefully treats the addict with as much love as possible and works jointly as a team to help him in his recovery. Then it would be time to tell him the boundaries you have come up with and the consequences should they be crossed.

Every home with an addict is distinctive in relating with each other, their upbringing, and personalities. What are healthy boundaries to you? What would you like to establish as boundaries? Here are some examples I find helpful:

## MONEY

Often the most difficult for a mom. She feels like if her son is out there without money, he may use something dangerous or get into some sort of trouble. But we cannot forget how resourceful addicts are; they will always find a way, and the less you give money, the better for both of you. However, you must make this clear. Let your son know that you have decided not to give him any money, but he would get a roof over his head, food to eat, and basic necessities. If he needs something to buy, you will get it yourself or some other responsible family member. This may not go well, but he must know it is a decision you have made without arguments or accusations. Every member of the family must be on board with this. He may get angry, accusing, or insulting, but you must remain composed and refuse to be drawn into an argument, paving the way for the next boundary.

## USE OF PROPER LANGUAGE

As a mother, you have a right to be treated with respect. It's possible that things have got out of hand, and your son has said words he should not say to you. Let him know that disrespectful or insulting language will not be acceptable from him or anyone in the home. Now I am assuming that people typically do not disrespect each other using curse words in your home. If they do, it may be a good idea for everyone to learn respect for each other. In the event he uses any foul language, let him know what the consequences would involve. This substantially depends on the age of your son and the type of language used in the home.

## ADDICT FRIENDS UNWELCOME

Except for some behavioral addictions where most addicts prefer their own company, substance abusers always have 'friends' whose commonality is the substance they use. In this case, if such friends had been visiting your son, then it's time to let him know that they are no longer welcome. Your goal is to have him surround himself with healthy people, so the more he is encouraged to spend time with those who can motivate and influence him positively, the less influential the other friends will be.

## NO DRUGS IN THE HOUSE

I have often seen moms displaying substances they found in their sons' rooms while cleaning. They are often unsure what they are, and it drives them crazy to imagine their child is using something more dangerous than what they already suspect. Setting boundaries in this area includes letting him know that if drugs are found in the house, they will be destroyed. It is unnecessary to waste your days looking for stash, as it just causes you unnecessary anxiety. All the same, he would have to look for another place to store his stash. Ideally, all substances should be eliminated from the home so that he does not justify his actions. If you tell him not to drink in your home and have wine every night, that might not go so well. Your son expects you to practice what you preach, and therefore all temptations should be eliminated.

## NO COVER-UPS OR DEFENDING A WRONG

Sometimes moms are afraid to let children face the consequences of their actions; if he misses school or work because he blacked out or slept late last night, then he should face the consequences coming to him. Let him know that you cannot cover or make excuses for him. If he gets arrested, he should also know that it's a consequence. It is hard to watch your son suffer in jail, and I don't believe it is the appropriate rehab for addicts. Ideally, they should be rehabilitated in a more humane environment seeing that they are often very unbalanced emotionally and mentally. Unfortunately, if he is caught in possession or robbing someone, he would be arrested, and that's just how the system works. You want to help him before things get entirely out of hand and he is no longer under your control.

## QUALITY FAMILY TIME

It is possible that you like having your family together for meals or activities. Your son may have been making excuses but encourage him to be present. For example, if you were used to saving him a plate for dinner and he would come to eat when others were done, let him know that you will no longer allow that. He must be home for meals or no meals at all, the same thing with family activities. You shouldn't miss an important meeting because he overslept or did not come home in time the night before. It would also be appropriate to let him know that he should be home at certain hours not to interrupt others who are already asleep or resting.

## NO ENABLING

Having boundaries ensures that the enabling stops. Enabling is a word that is often misused when connected with addiction, but while some things moms do are enabling, supporting your son in his recovery is not enabling. Enabling is like buying his affection, doing more for him than you would do under normal circumstances, often out of obligation or guilt. For example, giving him money knowing he will use it to support his behavior is enabling, and the reasons why moms do this vary. It could be a misguided belief that giving him what he wants will change him, and instead, he gets worse and becomes manipulative and entitled.

If you have been doing it and feel unable to stop, you will get the hang of it when you set boundaries and keep at them, and you will also gain some semblance of control when dealing with him. The line between helping and enabling your son is fine. As moms, we find it easier to do everything and support him in all ways just to avoid confrontations and arguments. But what are some of the things you can do without enabling him?

Since he is a teen or a young adult, you still provide for his education and all the basic things that a parent provides. You provide emotional support, acceptance, prayers, and positive reinforcements.

Or say your son is over 20 years old and has an apartment, you may realize that he is struggling to keep it together and work because he slips sometimes. Would you support him if he asks? Well, yes, but it also depends on the effort he puts in. Unfortunately, you cannot give him money if the rent is overdue. If he is facing eviction, pay the money yourself and let him know it is a loan. Your support is what he needs, and there are many ways to go about it without enabling.

It can be very draining to spend your time worrying about your son when he is in active addiction. Setting these boundaries will let him know that there will be consequences depending on what you find suitable.

At a subconscious level, you are also teaching him to take responsibility for his recovery. It may not seem like it, but this is an essential step. So, share a lot of love and positivity as you set your boundaries. When stated in a matter-of-fact tone without any accusations, criticisms, and judgments, you are conveying you are still in charge and still the parent.

It may be possible that you cannot tell him all the boundaries you have set up, but you must address this issue when you get another chance. Alternatively, you can write them down and hand them over. Some boundaries may not be verbalized, like if you decide not to engage in an argument, you simply don't. If your son comes home and you sense he is high, and you know he gets triggered easily when like that, the wise thing to do is avoid having a conversation that is triggering. But if he still wants to fight, then it's time to back off. Any angry exchange of words like we have agreed before would neither draw you closer nor help in his recovery, but it will spoil your mood, worsen your relationship, and mess up your sleep.

Boundaries are not about putting up walls of separation between you and your son, they are a way of creating respect for each other and your property. When your son realizes you love him despite his behavior and are denying him out of love and a need to rebuild trust, there begins a shift in how he views you and the world in general. Remember, you, the mom, are usually the first target of his anger, so you are the one to help him bridge the gap and heal your relationship.

Your son may not like the boundaries that you have to set up, but it is what he needs from you. Children, whatever their age, recognize authority, especially from a consistent parent. While setting them, it is imperative that he knows that you would hold him accountable. If the agreement is to put away used dishes or wash them, he should be reminded. Reminders without being nagging let him know that you consider him responsible. Consistency also makes him recognize you are the adult and the parent. He may not do all you ask, but you must continue to ask and expect.

If your son steals something, whether money, devices, or anything to sell to finance his habit, he should know what the consequences are. It pains me to imagine this, but even kicking him out of the family home may be a consequence. However, you will be the one reaching out more as boys tend to shut down and disappear. This way, you can recognize positive behavior and desire for change sooner, thus using the wedge for second chances.

# STEP #6

## HEAL THE TRAUMA, HEAL THE ADDICTION

# 19

# HEALING IN RELATIONSHIPS

The *7 Steps to Help Your Son in Addiction Recovery* is not a one-time read. There are practical tips that you will go back to several times to help improve your relationship with God, yourself, and your son. The awareness that you both might have experienced trauma may have made you more sensitive to the healing and recovery process. As we had seen earlier,

---

*"It is almost impossible to be a drug addict without having a prior history of childhood trauma."*

— BESSEL VAN DER KOLK

---

So, have you stopped asking questions like 'Why can't you just stop?' or 'Why are you doing this when your life isn't even that hard?' These questions not only make your son feel worthless but extremely guilty and ashamed for the trouble he has caused, which often leads him to further indulge in the world of addictions.

While you are not expected to become your son's therapist or psychologist, you may have communicated that possible trauma may have led to his addiction. Or maybe you are still not sure what happened. Either way, Dr. Bruce Perry, an American Psychiatrist, says that our relationships are where trauma occurs, as does the healing. He says that *healthy relationships are the agents of change, and the most powerful therapy is human love.* He added that some mental health professionals used to teach that people must love themselves first before anyone would love them; even those living with no social support could be psychologically healthy. While this may sound plausible, the truth is you must have experienced love to know how to love yourself. One cannot live in isolation and build the capacity to love.

You may have experienced love from God, your parents, relatives, teachers, your high school sweetheart, husband, or children, and you remember how that felt. Maybe you went to visit your best friend, and she listened, comforted you, and you felt loved. Either way, love is an essential tool for healthy relationships.

God, as our Creator, knows us intimately; yet he allows us to choose life with Him or death without Him. As much as He loves us, He does not impose Himself on humanity; instead, He reveals His glory and leaves us to decide which relationship we prefer. He is said to be a relational being. Besides the God Head, heaven is full of thousands and thousands of angels.

> "And I beheld, and I heard the voice of many angels round about the throne and the beasts and the elders: and the number of them was ten thousand times ten thousand, and thousands of thousands."

> — REVELATION 5:11

Then He created man,

> "And The Lord God said, it is not good that man should be alone; I will make him an help meet for him,"

> — GENESIS 2:19

and He created a woman and officiated the first marriage, He told them to multiply, thus paving the way for relationships in families. Further in the Bible, you may have noticed that most families were very dysfunctional, right from the very first one of Adam and Eve. Cain killed his brother and thus started a series of traumatic events. So, we can safely agree that trauma in families has occurred through generations, and humanity is destroying itself only stayed by God's power.

There are core traits to consider in healthy relationships. They include trust, value, and respect to allow for connections, encourage safety and growth, security, partnerships, self-responsibility, joy, and a sense of belonging. Some qualities included in these core traits include healthy communication and stability, intimacy, emotional closeness, and trust. People who hug, cuddle, touch, and spend a lot of time together tend to have great relationships as they motivate each other to grow and improve without imposing their own beliefs. They also practice vulnerability where no one is afraid to express unhappiness or sadness because they will not face any criticism or judgment.

It is almost impossible to have these relationships if Christ is not the center of your heart. As Matthew clearly states,

> *"And because iniquity shall abound, the love of many shall wax cold."*

> — MATTHEW 24:12

People generally do not love each other the way God desires; everyone is going through one kind of struggle or another affecting how parents and children interact, causing a rift that is sometimes not fixable. However, reducing stress and conflict despite the hostile environment is entirely possible with a few adjustments.

I have felt the pain of mothers when their sons relapse, some more than 20 times before they finally make it or die. For the most part, it is because they go to rehab then return to the same toxic environment they had left behind. They do not feel safe, and their emotional wounds are still raw; the trauma is still real, and they go right back to the very claws they were trying to escape.

You feel exasperated? Well so does your son. That he even agreed to go to rehab is a positive sign, so we can safely agree that he hates his current life and desires to escape. But because some issues have not been addressed, recovery takes longer than it should, and the cycle seems never-ending.

When the home environment feels secure and relationships healthier and happier, your son may quit the addiction without rehab or therapy. Dr. Marc Lewis, a developmental neuroscientist who disagrees with the disease model, is an example of a person who quit without rehab. He tells of his life in addiction and how he quit in his' Memoirs of an Addicted Brain.' According to him, addiction needs willpower and motivation to change. If your son desires to see you happy, meet a great girl to marry, or get an exciting job, that would motivate him to quit. Most people quit when they get married. The joy resulting from falling in love produces the chemical hormones that an addict craves, and this could be why people revert to addiction when the relationship goes sour. The insecurity brings back the fears that the user had experienced before.

My experience of identifying my son's trauma center may be different from your experience. Everyone has certain events, experiences, and adverse effects of an occurrence that might impact your son much later than expected. Due to the subjectivity of the issue, it's essential that you first understand your son and the type of person he was before the addiction kicked in.

# HEALING IN THERAPY

## NUTRITION THERAPY

You may wonder what nutrition has got to do with addiction. Well, most substance abusers ignore nutrition and often have a poor appetite, eat food with low or no nutrition, drink no water, and may experience damage to their organs or other health issues. Your son may prefer to grab a candy bar as opposed to preparing a healthy meal.

With the assumption that you oversee family meals, you can incorporate regular healthy meals by simply adding more nutrient-dense foods to reduce the poor or hard to digest foods like meats, cheese, dairy, and junk foods. By adding more plant-based foods like fruits and vegetables, you are helping a substance abuser detox and increasing the vitamins, minerals, and amino acids he needs.

Since plants are detoxifying in their nature, increasing them in your son's meals will help reduce cravings for addictive substances, detox to relieve the organs of their toxic load, and induce healing. It may not be easy to eliminate unhealthy food instantly; it can be done gradually by increasing the healthy and reducing the unhealthy options. Transitioning to a plant-based diet may be challenging, so purchasing a diet book would be helpful to find great recipes for the whole family to enjoy.

## MUSIC THERAPY

Generally speaking, music affects people on an emotional level. Music therapy has been helpful for Alzheimer's, Autism, and cancer patients; pain management, psychiatric hospitals, rehabs, and correctional centers. Research supports its effectiveness in emotional support, facilitating movement, and rehabilitation. It is known to be very effective for healing trauma. It's stimulating and relaxing, but one should be careful with the kind of music for therapy. Some music may be aggravating, causing unhealthy excitement instead of offering relaxation and relief. Hymns, for example, are said to be relaxing; an hour of this often makes my spirit revive. When my thoughts start rioting, or I feel discouraged, sad, or unable to pray, I turn to hymn music.

## MASSAGE THERAPY

So as not to appear remiss, I will mention this essential therapy that works wonders for trauma and addiction recovery. The brain may forget psychological trauma, but the body remembers. A trauma survivor sometimes experiences sensations that must be addressed. Most addicts never experience loving touches. While in active use, they are either unlovable, aggressive, prickly, or repulsive. Not many people want to be close to them, giving them loving hugs and touches. So, they miss out on this necessary human contact.

People who have been assaulted sexually may not like being touched, so offering massage as therapy may sound counterintuitive. Still, gentle, loving, and firm human contact are where healing for the unseen wounds starts. On a psychological level, massage stimulates the parasympathetic nervous system and deactivates the sympathetic nervous system. It provides muscle tension relaxation, improves deep breathing, circulation, digestion, and calms the hypothalamus.

Massage therapists work with patients ensuring they trust them and are comfortable with pressure, music, position, and interpersonal touch, which is crucial for recovery from trauma. If your son had experienced a trauma that caused him to feel like he had no control over his body or that he could not speak up, in massage therapy, he is free to speak up without fear and express any discomfort. He has an opportunity to connect with the sensations he has been experiencing in response to past adversities.

## MOVEMENT

Movement or exercise has been known to heal trauma, reduce stress, induce better sleep, and reduce addiction. In an article written by Ryan Collins, when people experience a 'runner's high,' it's because of the release of endorphins. These are said to be neurotransmitters that help to relieve pain and stress.

Dopamine, serotonin, and norepinephrine are other hormones that are positively impacted by regular movement. They help boost one's mood and provide a sense of well-being. If your son can be motivated to join in activities where he moves more, encourage him to join. If there is an activity he loved before, motivate him to pick it up again. Besides improving your relationship, his brain will produce the same chemicals he craves, reducing the desire for unhealthy options. What kind of movement can you adopt? Is it sports, mowing, skiing, hiking, gardening? And what about your son?

Besides these therapies, other self-care practices, including deep breathing, and stretching, reawaken the body's memory of intentional and loving touch.

## REHAB

It is very probable that your goal all along has been for your son to go to rehab. You may have been preparing for this moment, and now that it is here, and he has said he is ready, you should be prepared with places in mind that you can recommend to your son. He must take the initiative to call, plan the trip, and let you know how to support him. This is a huge decision depending on how far gone he was. So the whole family must be on board and supportive; he should never feel alone on this recovery journey. When he gets out of rehab, there should be plans in place for the second phase. The home environment must feel secure and healthy, and he should not stay idle. Does he want to get a job, go back to school, college or pursue a relationship? When he is motivated enough to get his life in order, he may not need to follow up with professional therapy. Again, it depends on how well he is doing and how deep he was in addiction, and the drugs he was using. Some drugs may not require rehab, but alcohol, opiates, and heroin require medical interventions because the withdrawal symptoms are brutal and can be fatal. Surprisingly cigarettes are among the most problematic drugs to quit.

## TRAUMA-FOCUSED COGNITIVE-BEHAVIORAL THERAPY (TF-CBT)

Professionals have investigated novel treatments ranging from neurofeedback, meditation, sports, and spiritual practices, which provide new avenues that activate the brain's natural neuroplasticity. They have found them to be successful in recovery from trauma.

Trauma-Focused Cognitive Behavioral Therapy (TF-CBT) is also recommended for those recovering from addiction and trauma. TF-CBT is a conjoint parent-child talk therapy that is evidence-based, and explores traumatic experiences they have faced, and seeks to help them heal their trauma.

The stages of Trauma-focused CBT are stabilization, trauma narration, processing, integration, and consolidation. This therapy may help your son tackle and process the complex distorted beliefs he cannot make sense of and provide skills to live everyday life. It helps him identify where to project the issues and triggers instead of substance abuse or self-harm.

The therapy will ensure your son can handle the truth regarding his trauma and embrace it. He will learn to trust you as a safe refuge, and you will learn to cope with the emotional distress you have experienced and be the rock your son needs. This therapy includes role-playing to help him prepare for any future encounters that might be problematic. Your son shall know what to do or how to react during a few of the potential occurrences that might trigger long-forgotten trauma and lead him to relapse.

# STEP #7

NEWSTART

# STOP THE GENERATIONAL CYCLE

*"Never will the human heart know happiness until it is submitted to be molded by the Spirit of God."*

— ELLEN G WHITE

We can agree by now that you cannot recover from addictions without recovering from trauma, and according to Dr. Bussel Van Der Kolk, *"Trauma victims cannot recover until they become familiar with and befriend the sensations in their bodies."* Awareness of physical sensations like tension, empty feelings, tingling, heat, and coldness may define how their bodies respond to the trauma they experienced in relation to the environment around them. So, if your son is not erupting in anger or doesn't seem as cold, distant, tense, or easily triggered, he is on the way to recovery. Therefore, it is important not to end the recovery process at rehab and therapy but to take a step further and stop the generational cycle.

For maximum results, these steps need to be repeated several times to adapt them into a lifestyle that will change your life, that of your son and his future children.

The lifestyle changes help you keep growing in values. While moral values need to be instilled at a young age, teens, young adults, and moms can still adopt new behaviors just like anybody else. A religious faith where Christ is the center is a good start. My greatest regret was not raising my son with Christian values and teaching him the importance of having a great love relationship with God.

It is quite possible that as you were reflecting in chapter twelve, you vividly saw yourself, a parent, an older sibling, or any relative who has struggled with one type of addiction or another. How often was it addressed? Growing up, I do not remember anyone discussing this elephant in the room, and it seemed like a normal part of life. I have seen many relatives addicted to alcohol and cigarettes without any attempt at interventions. Then their children became addicts, and people wondered why they did not learn from their parent's mistakes. But as we have learned so far, addiction beats logic unless one is willing to study the science behind it.

But how do you stop the generational cycle?

When God gave the ten commandments on Mount Sinai, He said in the third commandment,

> "...for I The Lord thy God am a jealous God, visiting the iniquity of the fathers upon the children unto the third and fourth generation of them that hate me; and shewing mercy unto thousands of them that love me, and keep my commandments."
>
> — EXODUS 20:5-6

Simply put, this scripture tells us that if we refuse to turn back to God in repentance, Satan will continue ruining families for generations until someone rises above the ruins, turns to God, and saves the family. We know from Bible history that a family can gain protection or favor because of one faithful family member. Could this be you?

Granted, it's not humanly possible to stop traumatic experiences from happening. There are a lot of Christian homes where they happen, and we see children of ministers, and other faithful members, succumbing to substance abuse. We are all human, and we may not all have a Christlike spirit as expected. For the most part, we have failed as parents and lost sight of the most precious things God gifted us with, our children. Satan has made us so busy that we spend more time away than with our children, and sometimes we are not aware of what is happening in our absence.

I read a story of a certain mom who left her son with a nanny when working. She believed he was safe only to learn one year later that the nanny had another job and would leave her son alone for hours and run back before the mom came back, all the while pretending that she had been with the boy all along. This neglect was traumatic to the baby boy, and it affected his social life and later on his teenage life when he became an uncontrollably violent addict. The mother had no way of knowing of this neglect until she came home early one day, found her infant son alone, and got a confession from the nanny. If this mom knew the long-term effects of neglect, she would have stayed home with her son, showered him with love and attention, teaching him to love, trust, obey God and her until he healed from the trauma. But she had no idea; she fired that nanny and got another one.

My son is an only child, so I do not have the opportunity to do this again yet. But maybe you have other young kids or grandkids. What do you intend to do differently?

My favorite writer Ellen White said that training children is the grandest work that was committed to humanity. They belong to God, and our job is to train them for him. Our pain from their bad habits is a result of our disobedience and neglect of duty. But God has given us the sure promise that we can turn this cycle around and save our children by taping on the greater power available.

I honestly cannot think of any other power besides The Word of God. It is full of promises for our good. Jesus spent more time healing than preaching.

*"And Jesus went about all Galilee, teaching in their*
*synagogues, and preaching the gospel of the*
*kingdom, and healing all manner of sickness*
*and all manner of disease among the people."*

— MATTHEWS 4:23

He is ready and willing to heal and save us.

Parents were chosen to represent God to their children and are held accountable for how they turn out. Moms especially have a special task of training, refining, and molding their children's character after the character of God. If the home becomes the happiest place on earth for them, where God is the center, then this cycle is destroyed, and that is a guarantee. God has promised, and His word, which never changes, says,

*"That our sons may be as plants grown up in their*
*youth; that our daughters may be as corner*
*stones polished after the similitude of a palace."*

— PSALM 144:12

He removes the dross, and the process is painful, but what is left behind? Gold refined by fire.

A Newstart does not mean smooth sailing without storms ever; it simply means that you have made some significant changes and are willing to follow through from today. Although you may be highly explicit and intentional about your expectations of your recovering son's behavioral changes, you may be flexible in how he makes these critical adjustments. Understand there is no harm in adopting his approaches to change things if the process obtains similar results. So, allow your boy the benefit of the doubt and let him gain the freedom to do it his way, trusting in the omnipotent power. Motivating him to adopt healthy practices and envision a future free of addiction but full of purpose and joy.

With new purpose is a new beginning; after every storm, a new day begins. With a new cycle, new lifestyle adaptations, a new start for both your lives and the lives of other children in the family begins. Are there changes you would be willing to make for the sake of your family, your son's siblings, or future children?

What better way than to help them acknowledge the power of God and the role He plays in the recovery of your son from addiction? With a Newstart comes new hopes and goals.

# THE 12 STEPS

The 12 steps are a culmination of the Newstart. These steps started as the guiding principles of a mutual self-help group called Alcoholics Anonymous. Abstinence, fellowship with others, and surrender to a spiritual higher power were solutions discovered by the founders. Your son can personalize these steps and make them his own, and he can learn more from going to the Source, The Word of God.

**Step 1**: I admit I was powerless over sinful addictive habits, and my path was leading me to destruction.
*Admitting that something has been wrong in my life will let me acknowledge the truth.*

**Step 2**: I now believe God will restore me.
*I trust my strength and safety in the arms of God.*

**Step 3**: I decided to let Jesus into my heart to mold me according to His will.
*I acknowledged God as my only helper.*

**Step 4**: I had moments of soul searching and reflecting on my past sinful habits.
*I reflected on my life and acknowledged that I hurt myself, others and made poor decisions.*

**Step 5**: I saw my sins, repented, and confessed them to God and loved ones.
*I account for the wrongs I did and ask for forgiveness.*

**Step 6**: I prayed for Christ to cleanse and cover me with His righteousness.
*I have found a friend closer than a brother.*

**Step 7**: I humbly ask Jesus. to make me as white as snow
*I submit to God and trust him to help.*

**Step 8**: I have reflected and listed all persons I had hurt, and I am willing to ask for forgiveness.
*I acknowledge and take responsibility for the bridges I burnt and the people I hurt.*

**Step 9**: I will treat others as I would like to be treated.
*Taking action and treating others as Christ would treat them, with love and kindness, to rebuild broken relationships.*

**Step 10**: I must continue to walk on the right path, and when I veer off, I will promptly get back on track, take notes and seek help.
*The Spirit of God helps me watch my behavior and prevents me from doing things that ruin my relationship with Him and others.*

**Step 11**: Through prayer and meditation, I sought to keep in contact with God, praying only to know His will and give me the power to overcome temptations.
*This step proves to me my progress spiritually and mentally.*

**Step 12**: Jesus said in Matthew 10 verse 8, "...freely ye have received, freely give. I have had a spiritual awakening and intend to share with other addicts my good news and practice all the steps.
*The word and works of God cannot be hidden under a bushel; I will share with others the testimony of the victory I have received to the best of my ability.*

# CONCLUSION

This book was not merely a book but a journey. One that I believe you can complete with your son as you guide him to recovery. Only a mom can understand the pain of a mom. So, I intended to understand yours and help you in this marathon. I trust I was able to do some good and bring some hope to your life. If this book has helped even one single mother, I will consider myself successful.

We have discussed various techniques and ways you can help yourself as well as your son. I sincerely hope that by now, you understand your son's struggle better, and what he could be going through, and the importance of your role is in his recovery.

I would love it if you could discuss what you learned with your friends, family, or support groups and compare notes.

Before you know it, your life will turn around in ways you never thought possible.

God Bless You!

## Please leave a review

But before you go, I have one final question, have you enjoyed this book? I genuinely hope so! Your valuable feedback would help me produce quality books and help other moms looking for books like these. If you would just take a minute or two to share your thoughts about it, that would mean a great deal to me.

Please search for the book on Amazon and leave a review.

Thank you!

# REFERENCES

1. Patry, E., Bratberg, J. P., Buchanan, A., Paiva, A. L., Balestrieri, S., & Matson, K. L. (2019). Rx for addiction and medication safety: An evaluation of teen education for opioid misuse prevention. Research in Social and Administrative Pharmacy, 15(8), 917-924.
2. Substance Abuse and Mental Health Services Administration. (2017). Key substance use and mental health indicators in the United States: Results from the 2016 National Survey on Drug Use and Health. HHS Publication No. SMA 17-5044, NSDUH Series H-52.
3. Moustafa, A. A., Parkes, D., Fitzgerald, L., Underhill, D., Garami, J., Levy-Gigi, E., ... & Misiak, B. (2021). The relationship between childhood trauma, early-

life stress, and alcohol and drug use, abuse, and addiction: An integrative review. Current Psychology, 40(2), 579-584.

4. (2017). Brainfacts.org.

5. Maté, G. (2012). Addiction: Childhood trauma, stress and the biology of addiction. Journal of Restorative Medicine, 1(1), 56-63.

6. Dr. Gabor Maté on how addiction changes the brain- https://www.youtube.com/watch?v=UTML66Hv4vc

7. De Bellis MD, Baum AS, Birmaher B, Keshavan MS, Eccard CH, Boring AM, Jenkins FJ, Ryan ND. A.E. Bennett Research Award. Developmental traumatology.Part I: Biological stress systems. Biol Psychiatry. 1999,45(10):1259–1270.

8. Vythilingam M, Heim C, Newport J, Miller AH, Anderson E, Bronen R, Brummer M, Staib L, VermettenE, Charney DS, Nemeroff CB, Bremner JD. Childhood trauma associated with smaller hippocampal volume in women with major depression. Am J Psychiatry. 2002, 159(12): 2072–2080.

9. Washtenaw. (n.d.). *Know the risks* [Review of *Know the risks*]. Washtenaw.org. https://www.washtenaw.org/DocumentCenter/View/5548/Suicide-Attempt-Data-Presentation-2015-PDF know the risk; increase hope

10. Volkow, N. D., Fowler, J. S., Wang, G. J., Swanson, J.

M., & Telang, F. (2007). Dopamine in drug abuse and addiction: results of imaging studies and treatment implications. Archives of neurology, 64(11), 1575-1579.

11. Abuse, S., US, M. H. S. A., & Office of the Surgeon General (US. (2016). THE NEUROBIOLOGY OF SUBSTANCE USE, MISUSE, AND ADDICTION. In Facing Addiction in America: The Surgeon General's Report on Alcohol, Drugs, and Health [Internet]. US Department of Health and Human Services.

12. Evren, C., Cınar, O., Evren, B., & Celik, S. (2011). History of suicide attempt in male substance-dependent inpatients and relationship to borderline personality features, anger, hostility, and aggression. Psychiatry Research, 190(1), 126-131.

13. https://ndarc.med.unsw.edu.au/blog/yes-people-can-die-opiate-withdrawal

14. Widyanto, L., & Griffiths, M. (2006). 'Internet addiction': a critical review. International Journal of mental health and Addiction, 4(1), 31-51.

15. Lewis, M. (2017). Addiction and the Brain: Development, Not Disease. *Neuroethics, 10*(1), 7–18.

16. *THE COMMON SENSE CENSUS: MEDIA USE BY TWEENS AND TEENS.* (2019).

17. (2021). Apa.org. https://www.apa.org/gradpsych/features/2011/cell-phone-addiction

18. Ekern, J. (2017, April 2). *PTSD, Eating Disorders and Trauma.* Eating Disorder Hope.

19. Recovery First Treatment Center. "The Connection between Eating Disorders and Addiction." *Recovery First Treatment Center*, 19 Mar. 2019

20. *Strict parenting actually creates behavior problems in children. Here's why.* (n.d.). Markham, Dr. L. (n.d.). *What's wrong with strict parenting?* Aha! Parenting; Laura Markham.

21. Mayo Clinic. (2016). Compulsive gambling - Symptoms and causes.

22. *Is It Retail Therapy? Or Do You Have a Shopping Compulsion?* (2015, November 20). Health Essentials from Cleveland Clinic.

23. *The Impact of Work Addiction on Well-being.* (2020, February 10). University of Nevada, Reno.

24. *How to Understand the Phenomenon of Food Addiction.* (n.d.). Verywell Mind.

25. Garami, J., Valikhani, A., Parkes, D., Haber, P., Mahlberg, J., Misiak, B., ... & Moustafa, A. A. (2019). Examining perceived stress, childhood trauma, and interpersonal trauma in individuals with drug addiction. Psychological Reports, 122(2), 433-450.

26. Baksh, J., LMHC, MCAP, & Officer, C. C. (2019, August 26). *Mother of Drug Addicted Son Shares Her Story.* Foundations Wellness Center.

27. Zou, Z., Wang, H., Uquillas, F. D. O., Wang, X., Ding, J., & Chen, H. (2017). Definition of substance and non-substance addiction. Substance and Non-substance Addiction, 21-41.

28. Koob, G. F., & Volkow, N. D. (2010). Neurocircuitry of addiction. Neuropsychopharmacology, 35(1), 217-238.

29. Maté, G. (2008). In the realm of hungry ghosts: Close encounters with addiction. Random House Digital, Inc.

30. Gupta, S., & Kulhara, P. (2007). Cellular and molecular mechanisms of drug dependence: An overview and update. Indian journal of psychiatry, 49(2), 85.

31. Virkkunen, M., Rawlings, R., Tokola, R., Poland, R. E., Guidotti, A., Nemeroff, C., ... & Linnoila, M. (1994). CSF biochemistries, glucose metabolism, and diurnal activity rhythms in alcoholic, violent offenders, fire setters, and healthy volunteers. Archives of general psychiatry, 51(1), 20-27.

32. Sharma, S. K., Klee, W. A., & Nirenberg, M. (1975). Dual regulation of adenylate cyclase accounts for narcotic dependence and tolerance. Proceedings of the National Academy of Sciences, 72(8), 3092-3096.

33. National Institute on Drug Abuse, 2021. *Cannabis use may be associated with suicidality in young adults/ National Institute On Drug Abuse* [online]

34. Nestler, E. J. (2005). The neurobiology of cocaine addiction. Science & practice perspectives, 3(1), 4.

35. Deval, G., 2021. *Evidence that spanking alters the brain.* [online] PARENTING SCIENCE.

36. Drug Rehab Options. 2021. *Sexual Trauma and*

*Addiction: Understanding Child Sexual Abuse and Drug Use - Drug Rehab Options*. American Addiction Centers

37. Van der Kolk, B. A., & McFarlane, A. C. (Eds.). (1996). Traumatic stress: The effects of overwhelming experience on mind, body, and society. Guilford Press.

38. Schwartz, J. M., & Begley, S. (2009). The mind and the brain. Springer Science & Business Media.

39. Bellis, M. A., Hardcastle, K., Ford, K., Hughes, K., Ashton, K., Quigg, Z., & Butler, N. (2017). Does continuous trusted adult support in childhood impart life-course resilience against adverse childhood experiences-a retrospective study on adult health-harming behaviors and mental well-being. BMC psychiatry, 17(1), 1-12.

40. *Setting Appropriate Boundaries With The Addict*. (2021, January 26). Peaks Recovery Centers.

41. "Healthy Relationships." *Rehab Spot*, Rehab Spot, 18 Aug. 2021,

42. Collins, R. (2017, July 26). *Exercise, Depression, and the Brain*. Healthline.

43. *Touch for Trauma*. (2018, November 5). MassageTherapy.Com.

44. Team, E. (2019, May 6). *Music Therapy for Trauma| Training for Music Therapists*. Chiropractor Resources, Chiropractic Techniques, Chiropractic Advice.

45. The Muse. 2021. *The 24/6 Life: How 1 Day Off Can Help Your Career.*

46. Trauma-Focused Cognitive Behavioral Therapy: A primer for child https://www.childwelfare.gov/pubpdfs/trauma.pdf

47. *The Faith I Live By-* Ellen G. White Writings